Political Science
Institutions and Public Policy

Sherri Mora

Patricia Caperton Parent

Texas State University ● San Marcos

Kendall Hunt
publishing company

Kendall Hunt
publishing company

www.kendallhunt.com
Send all inquiries to:
4050 Westmark Drive
Dubuque, IA 52004-1840

Contents

CHAPTER **4** Texas Politics **89**

CHAPTER **9** Civil Liberties and Affirmative Action ...**161**

CHAPTER **10** Immigration **175**

CHAPTER **11** Foreign Policy **183**

Acknowledgments

Thanks to William England for putting this project together, Abigail Brittain for her hard work on a tight deadline, Denise Bjerke for her insightful contributions, and Greg Derosa for his creative solutions.

CHAPTER

1 American Political System

THEORETICAL FOUNDATIONS

Elements of a State

What does it mean to be a state? Generally when we capitalize the word state (State), we are referring to a nation. Most agree that nations share defining characteristics that include the following:

- **Territory**
  - The land a State controls, with defined boundaries and distinct, recognizable features

- **Population**
  - No specific number of inhabitants required, but there must be sufficient numbers in order for the State to be self-sustaining

- **Government**
  - Some form of political organization or government by which public policy is formulated and the affairs of State are conducted

- **Sovereignty**
  - ○ The power and authority to enact and enforce its laws; relatively free from external control by other nations
- **Recognition**
  - ○ Acknowledgement of a State's existence and sovereign authority by other nations within the global community

The Role of Government

Government is a form of political organization that enacts public policy and administers the affairs of the State. Our view of government and what it should do has changed over time. Throughout the centuries, political philosophers have expressed a variety of views about the nature of government.

Plato	Aristotle

• Viewed man as a rational being in a rational universe.
• Ideal form of government could be discovered through the exercise of human reason.
• Described the nation-state as consisting of a ruling class, a warrior class, and a working class.
• Justice prevailed when each class worked at its particular task and refrained from interfering with the work of others.
• Political authority was based on exact knowledge, thus rulers were not lawmakers.
• Law, based on custom and tradition, had no place in Plato's ideal state since it represented little more than an opinion of the truth.
	• "Father of Political Science."
	• Used the concept of human reasoning to analyze nation-states that existed in his time.
	• Man is political by nature and must participate in the governance of the State to be truly human.
	• Categorized forms of government or political organization as being good or bad, depending on who benefited from government's action.
	• Forms of government included:
	  • Government by the one
	  • Government by the few
	  • Government by the many

Aristotle's Classification of Government				
Aristotle's Classification of Government	Goal of Government	Rule by One	Rule by Few	Rule by Many
Good	To benefit the community	Monarchy	Aristocracy	Constitutional form
Bad	To benefit those that rule	Tyrant	Oligarchy	Democracy

John Locke

- Conceived of government as a means of securing individual rights—namely life, liberty, and property.
- Social Contract—Men were not political by nature; they consented to be governed for the purpose of protecting their rights.
- Participation in government is not necessary for human fulfillment but at a method for securing liberty.
- Goal of government is the protection of the individual.

Charles de Secondat, Baron de Montequieu

- Concerned with the concentration of power.
- Argued that power concentrated in any individual or single institution was oppressive.
- To prevent tyranny and to secure liberty, power should be separated.

Summary Table

PHILOSOPHER	VIEW OF MAN	GOAL OF GOVERNMENT	SEMINAL WORK
Plato	Rational by nature	Rule in accordance with Truth	The Republic
Aristotle	Must participate directly in government	Virtuous republic	Politics
Locke	Willing to submit to social contract	Secure liberty	Two Treatises of Government
Montesquieu	Concerned about the concentration of power	Secure liberty by separation of power	The Spirit of the Laws

Systems of Government

A system of government represents the larger view of a political organization that illustrates how different levels of government within a nation interact. We can explore this interaction in terms of how power and authority are distributed within the system. Intergovernmental relations refer to the entire set of interactions between and among national, state, and local governments. There are three major systems of government:

- **Unitary**
  - Formal authority rests with the national government.
  - Power in lower levels of government is prescribed by national directive.

○ Most governments in the world today have a unitary system (e.g., United Kingdom).

- **Confederation**
  ○ National government is created by and derives its authority from the member states.
  ○ Prior to the ratification of the United States Constitution, the U.S. system of government was a confederation.
  ○ A contemporary example of this type of system would be the European Union (EU) with its 27 member nations. The institutions of the EU perform specific functions based on agreement by its members.

- **Federal**
  ○ A constitutional division of power exists between the nation and the states, in which each level of government enforces its laws directly on its citizens.
  ○ The United States of America has a federal system.

How Power Flows		
UNITARY SYSTEM	**CONFEDERATION**	**FEDERAL SYSTEM**
National Government	Member States	National Government
↓	↓	↓ ↑
Local Governments	Central Government	State Governments

Informative Websites

http://classics.mit.edu/Aristotle/politics.html
Aristotle's *Politics*

http://europa.eu/index_en.htm
European Union Official Site

http://avalon.law.yale.edu/18th_century/fed39.asp
The Federalist Papers: No. 39 (explaining the federal form of government)

http://www.uoregon.edu/~rbear/hobbes/leviathan.html
Hobbes's *Leviathan*

http://www.fordham.edu/halsall/mod/1690locke-sel.html
Locke's *Two Treatises of Government*

http://www.fordham.edu/halsall/mod/montesquieu-spirit.html
Montesquieu's *The Spirit of the Laws*

http://www.direct.gov.uk/en/Governmentcitizensandrights/UKgovernment/
Centralgovernmentandthemonarchy/DG_073438
Official Overview of Government in the United Kingdom

http://classics.mit.edu/Plato/republic.html
Plato's *The Republic*

http://www.constitution.org/jjr/socon.htm
Rousseau's *The Social Contract*

EXERCISE 1

List and explain the three systems of government.

EXERCISE 2

Draw a chart of our current system of government and include notations that indicate each philosopher's influence.

ARTICLES OF CONFEDERATION

After declaring independence from England, the Thirteen Original Colonies entered into a form of government known as a confederation and crafted the Articles of Confederation, under which they became the United States of America. The Articles were in effect from 1781 to 1789. Notice the wording of the first three articles:

I. The Stile of this Confederacy shall be "**The United States of America**"

II. Each state retains its sovereignty, freedom, and independence, and every power, jurisdiction, and right, which is not by this Confederation expressly delegated to the United States, in Congress assembled.

III. The said States hereby severally enter into a firm league of friendship with each other, for their common defense, the security of their liberties, and their mutual and general welfare, binding themselves to assist each other, against all force offered to, or attacks made upon them, or any of them, on account of religion, sovereignty, trade, or any other pretense whatever.

The national government was very simplistic. It consisted of a single body, called the United States Congress, and was composed of delegates appointed annually by the legislature of each state. Every state had one vote regardless of its population. John Adams referred to it as nothing more than a "diplomatic assembly." No judicial branch existed to adjudicate disputes between the states, and no executive branch existed to coordinate the work of the central government.

Problems Under the Articles of Confederation

Congress Could Not:	State Governments
• Force states to meet military quotas. No standing army could be formed. • Regulate commerce. States erected barriers to trade that were harmful to economic progress. • Levy Taxes. National treasury was not well supplied.	• Each state remained independent and sovereign. • Excessively democratic • Powerful state legislatures

Laws were difficult to enact under the Articles of Confederation. Approval from nine of the thirteen states was necessary to approve legislation. Even if laws were passed, Congress had no power to enforce them. In addition, the Articles of Confederation were very rigid; they could only be amended by a unanimous vote.

In Massachusetts, an armed rebellion led by Daniel Shays ensued after a period of tax-raising legislation that favored the dominant merchant class and disadvantaged farmers. This event was so disconcerting to government officials that it marked a turning point in thinking about whether the government created under the Articles of Confederation was sufficient to serve the United States.

Informative Websites

http://avalon.law.yale.edu/18th_century/artconf.asp
  Articles of Confederation

http://oll.libertyfund.org/index.php?option=com_staticxt&staticfile=show.php?
  title=2098&Itemid=27
  The Works of John Adams

EXERCISES

EXERCISE 1

Draw a diagram that shows the structure of the United States under the Articles of Confederation, and indicate how the levels of government interact.

EXERCISE 2

Identify and discuss problems at the national level and the state level that resulted from the structure of government provided by the Articles.

CONSTITUTIONS

Constitutions are written to structure government, assign it power, and to limit its authority. Whether a constitution is liberal or restrictive depends on the amount of detail that is included about the actions government may take.

Liberal Versus Restrictive Constitutions			
TYPE	**STRUCTURE**	**POWER**	**LIMITATIONS**
Liberal	Provides the basic structure of government institutions.	Assigns government power without too much detail. Allows for broad legislative action.	Identifies specific limitations on government.
Restrictive	Provides a detailed plan for the structure of government's institutions.	Assigns government specific power in great detail. Legislative action is also detailed.	Identifies specific limitations on government.

Drafting Our Constitution: The Philadelphia Convention

Upon recognizing key problems with the Articles of Confederation, prominent individuals met to discuss options. These meetings led to the Constitutional Convention held in Philadelphia between May and September of 1787.

There were 55 delegates present in Philadelphia, including George Washington, who presided over the convention, and James Madison, who is considered the Father of the Constitution for his contributions. All those in attendance were politically savvy, wealthy, and well educated.

The purpose of the convention was to revise the Articles of Confederation. It became clear very early in the convention that a new form of government would result when all agreed to establish a national government with a supreme executive, legislative, and judicial branch.

Virginia Plan	New Jersey Plan	Connecticut Compromise

• Proposed by Edmund Randolph
• Favored large states and disadvantaged smaller states
• Bicameral legislature
  • Lower house apportioned by population
  • Upper house selected by the members of the lower house
	• Proposed by small states
	• Unicameral legislature
	• All states had equal representation regardless of population.
	• Very similar to the Articles of Confederation
		• Proposed by Roger Sherman of Connecticut
		• Also known as "Great Compromise"
		• Bicameral legislature
		  • Lower house apportioned by population
		  • Upper house based on equal representation
		  • This is the structure embodied in the Constitution today.

Many competing interests and sectional conflicts were addressed in the making of the U.S. Constitution:

- **Big states versus small states**
- **Northern states versus southern states**
- **Slave states versus free states**
- **Mercantile interests versus agrarian interests**

One of the most contentious matters was the issue of slavery. The founding fathers believed that it would have doomed the convention had they attempted to address this issue head on. Instead, the matter was dealt with in terms of practical application.

Southern states feared that a newly constituted government might prohibit slavery. This was not an unreasonable concern, as many found the practice of slavery abhorrent. To allay fears that slavery would be abolished, an agreement was reached in which the importation of slaves would not be banned prior to 1808. Concerns over how to count slaves for the purpose of representation also required a compromise. For the purpose of representation, every five slaves would be counted as three white citizens. This became know as the Three-Fifths Compromise.

Of all the compromises reached during the Constitutional Convention, the one that took the most time was how to structure and select the executive branch. The result was a single chief executive chosen by the electoral college. (This topic is discussed in Chapter 3).

What emerged from the convention in Philadelphia was truly an American innovation. Characteristics of the new liberal Republic included the following:

- **Popular sovereignty**
  - Political authority held in the hands of the people

- **Republicanism**
  - Representative form of government; one in which elected officials act on behalf of the people

- **Separation of powers**
  - Separation of the branches of government into an executive branch, a legislative branch, and a judicial branch

- **Checks and balances**
  - Each branch carries out its delegated powers but at the same time has some authority over other branches
  - *Example:* A presidential veto of legislation is a check on the legislative branch, and the Legislature's authority to impeach and remove a Justice is a check on the judicial branch.

- **Federalism**
  - Vertical division of power between the national government and the states

- **Limited government**
  - The Constitution specifies powers granted to government as well as powers that are restricted.
  - Important to insure against the unnecessary interference of government in people's lives and their pursuits

- **Supremacy of national law**
  - Unequivocally stated in the Constitution
  - In a contest between a state and the national government, the Constitution and laws passed by Congress are supreme.

All these characteristics were embodied within a dynamic Constitution written in sufficiently general terms to allow for interpretation over time.

THE CONSTITUTION OF THE UNITED STATES OF AMERICA

We the people of the United States, in order to form a more perfect union, establish justice, insure domestic tranquility, provide for the common defense, promote the general welfare, and secure the blessings of liberty to ourselves and our posterity, do ordain and establish this Constitution for the United States of America.

Article I

Section 1. All legislative powers herein granted shall be vested in a Congress of the United States, which shall consist of a Senate and House of Representatives.

Section 2. The House of Representatives shall be composed of members chosen every second year by the people of the several states, and the electors in each state shall have the qualifications requisite for electors of the most numerous branch of the state legislature.

No person shall be a Representative who shall not have attained to the age of twenty five years, and been seven years a citizen of the United States, and who shall not, when elected, be an inhabitant of that state in which he shall be chosen.

Representatives and direct taxes shall be apportioned among the several states which may be included within this union, according to their respective numbers, which shall be determined by adding to the whole number of free persons, including those bound to service for a term of years, and excluding Indians not taxed, three fifths of all other Persons. The actual Enumeration shall be made within three years after the first meeting of the Congress of the United States, and within every subsequent term of ten years, in such manner as they shall by law direct. The number of Representatives shall not exceed one for every thirty thousand, but each state shall have at least one Representative; and until such enumeration shall be made, the state of New Hampshire shall be entitled to chuse three, Massachusetts eight, Rhode Island and Providence Plantations one, Connecticut five, New York six, New Jersey four, Pennsylvania eight, Delaware one, Maryland six, Virginia ten, North Carolina five, South Carolina five, and Georgia three.

When vacancies happen in the Representation from any state, the executive authority thereof shall issue writs of election to fill such vacancies.

The House of Representatives shall choose their speaker and other officers; and shall have the sole power of impeachment.

Section 3. The Senate of the United States shall be composed of two Senators from each state, chosen by the legislature thereof, for six years; and each Senator shall have one vote.

Immediately after they shall be assembled in consequence of the first election, they shall be divided as equally as may be into three classes. The seats of the Senators of the first class shall be vacated at the expiration of the second year, of the second class at the expiration of the fourth year, and the third class at the expiration of the sixth year, so that one third may be chosen every second year; and if vacancies happen by resignation, or otherwise, during the recess of the legislature of any state, the executive thereof may make temporary appointments until the next meeting of the legislature, which shall then fill such vacancies.

No person shall be a Senator who shall not have attained to the age of thirty years, and been nine years a citizen of the United States and who shall not, when elected, be an inhabitant of that state for which he shall be chosen.

The Vice President of the United States shall be President of the Senate, but shall have no vote, unless they be equally divided.

The Senate shall choose their other officers, and also a President pro tempore, in the absence of the Vice President, or when he shall exercise the office of President of the United States.

The Senate shall have the sole power to try all impeachments. When sitting for that purpose, they shall be on oath or affirmation. When the President of the United States is tried, the Chief Justice shall preside: And no person shall be convicted without the concurrence of two thirds of the members present.

Judgment in cases of impeachment shall not extend further than to removal from office, and disqualification to hold and enjoy any office of honor, trust or profit under the United States: but the party convicted shall neverthe-less be liable and subject to indictment, trial, judgment and punishment, according to law.

Section 4. The times, places and manner of holding elections for Senators and Representatives, shall be prescribed in each state by the legislature thereof; but the Congress may at any time by law make or alter such regulations, except as to the places of choosing Senators.

The Congress shall assemble at least once in every year, and such meeting shall be on the first Monday in December, unless they shall by law appoint a different day.

Section 5. Each House shall be the judge of the elections, returns and qual-ifications of its own members, and a majority of each shall constitute a quorum to do business; but a smaller number may adjourn from day to day, and may be authorized to compel the attendance of absent members, in such manner, and under such penalties as each House may provide.

Each House may determine the rules of its proceedings, punish its members for disorderly behavior, and, with the concurrence of two thirds, expel a member.

Each House shall keep a journal of its proceedings, and from time to time publish the same, excepting such parts as may in their judgment require secrecy; and the yeas and nays of the members of either House on any question shall, at the desire of one fifth of those present, be entered on the journal.

Neither House, during the session of Congress, shall, without the consent of the other, adjourn for more than three days, nor to any other place than that in which the two Houses shall be sitting.

Section 6. The Senators and Representatives shall receive a compensation for their services, to be ascertained by law, and paid out of the treasury of the United States. They shall in all cases, except treason, felony and breach of the peace, be privileged from arrest during their attendance at the session of their respective Houses, and in going to and returning from the same; and for any speech or debate in either House, they shall not be questioned in any other place.

No Senator or Representative shall, during the time for which he was elected, be appointed to any civil office under the authority of the United States, which shall have been created, or the emoluments whereof shall have been increased during such time: and no person holding any office under the United States, shall be a member of either House during his continuance in office.

Section 7. All bills for raising revenue shall originate in the House of Represen-tatives; but the Senate may propose or concur with amendments as on other Bills.

Every bill which shall have passed the House of Representatives and the Senate, shall, before it become a law, be presented to the President of the United States; if he approve he shall sign it, but if not he shall return it, with his objections to that House in which it shall have originated, who shall enter the objections at large on their journal, and proceed to reconsider it. If after such reconsideration two thirds of that House shall agree to pass the bill, it shall be sent, together with the objec-tions, to the other House, by which it shall likewise be reconsidered, and if approved by two thirds of that House, it shall become a law. But in all such cases the votes of both Houses shall be determined by yeas and nays, and the names of the persons voting for and against the bill shall be entered on the journal of each House respectively. If any bill shall not be returned by the President within ten days

(Sundays excepted) after it shall have been presented to him, the same shall be a law, in like manner as if he had signed it, unless the Congress by their adjournment prevent its return, in which case it shall not be a law.

Every order, resolution, or vote to which the concurrence of the Senate and House of Representatives may be necessary (except on a question of adjournment) shall be presented to the President of the United States; and before the same shall take effect, shall be approved by him, or being disapproved by him, shall be repassed by two thirds of the Senate and House of Representatives, according to the rules and limitations prescribed in the case of a bill.

Section 8. The Congress shall have power to lay and collect taxes, duties, imposts and excises, to pay the debts and provide for the common defense and general welfare of the United States; but all duties, imposts and excises shall be uniform throughout the United States;

To borrow money on the credit of the United States;

To regulate commerce with foreign nations, and among the several states, and with the Indian tribes;

To establish a uniform rule of naturalization, and uniform laws on the subject of bankruptcies throughout the United States;

To coin money, regulate the value thereof, and of foreign coin, and fix the standard of weights and measures;

To provide for the punishment of counterfeiting the securities and current coin of the United States;

To establish post offices and post roads;

To promote the progress of science and useful arts, by securing for limited times to authors and inventors the exclusive right to their respective writings and discoveries;

To constitute tribunals inferior to the Supreme Court;

To define and punish piracies and felonies committed on the high seas, and offenses against the law of nations;

To declare war, grant letters of marque and reprisal, and make rules concerning captures on land and water;

To raise and support armies, but no appropriation of money to that use shall be for a longer term than two years;

To provide and maintain a navy;

To make rules for the government and regulation of the land and naval forces;

To provide for calling forth the militia to execute the laws of the union, suppress insurrections and repel invasions;

To provide for organizing, arming, and disciplining, the militia, and for governing such part of them as may be employed in the service of the United States, reserving to the states respectively, the appointment of the officers, and the authority of training the militia according to the discipline prescribed by Congress;

To exercise exclusive legislation in all cases whatsoever, over such District (not exceeding ten miles square) as may, by cession of particular states, and the acceptance of Congress, become the seat of the government of the United States, and to exercise like authority over all places purchased by the consent of the legislature of the state in which the same shall be, for the erection of forts, magazines, arsenals, dockyards, and other needful buildings;—And

To make all laws which shall be necessary and proper for carrying into execution the foregoing powers, and all other powers vested by this Constitution in the government of the United States, or in any department or officer thereof.

Section 9. The migration or importation of such persons as any of the states now existing shall think proper to admit, shall not be prohibited by the Congress prior to the year one thousand eight hundred and eight, but a tax or duty may be imposed on such importation, not exceeding ten dollars for each person.

The privilege of the writ of habeas corpus shall not be suspended, unless when in cases of rebellion or invasion the public safety may require it.

No bill of attainder or ex post facto Law shall be passed.

No capitation, or other direct, tax shall be laid, unless in proportion to the census or enumeration herein before directed to be taken.

No tax or duty shall be laid on articles exported from any state.

No preference shall be given by any regulation of commerce or revenue to the ports of one state over those of another: nor shall vessels bound to, or from, one state, be obliged to enter, clear or pay duties in another.

No money shall be drawn from the treasury, but in consequence of appropriations made by law; and a regular statement and account of receipts and expenditures of all public money shall be published from time to time.

No title of nobility shall be granted by the United States: and no person holding any office of profit or trust under them, shall, without the consent of the Congress, accept of any present, emolument, office, or title, of any kind whatever, from any king, prince, or foreign state.

Section 10. No state shall enter into any treaty, alliance, or confederation; grant letters of marque and reprisal; coin money; emit bills of credit; make anything but gold and silver coin a tender in payment of debts; pass any bill of attainder, ex post facto law, or law impairing the obligation of contracts, or grant any title of nobility.

No state shall, without the consent of the Congress, lay any imposts or duties on imports or exports, except what may be absolutely necessary for executing it's inspection laws: and the net produce of all duties and imposts, laid by any state on imports or exports, shall be for the use of the treasury of the United States; and all such laws shall be subject to the revision and control of the Congress.

No state shall, without the consent of Congress, lay any duty of tonnage, keep troops, or ships of war in time of peace, enter into any agreement or compact with another state, or with a foreign power, or engage in war, unless actually invaded, or in such imminent danger as will not admit of delay.

Article II

Section 1. The executive power shall be vested in a President of the United States of America. He shall hold his office during the term of four years, and, together with the Vice President, chosen for the same term, be elected, as follows:

Each state shall appoint, in such manner as the Legislature thereof may direct, a number of electors, equal to the whole number of Senators and Representatives to which the State may be entitled in the Congress: but no Senator or Representative, or person holding an office of trust or profit under the United States, shall be appointed an elector.

The electors shall meet in their respective states, and vote by ballot for two persons, of whom one at least shall not be an inhabitant of the same state with themselves. And they shall make a list of all the persons voted for, and of the number of votes for each; which list they shall sign and certify, and transmit sealed to the seat of the government of the United States, directed to the President of the Senate. The President of the Senate shall, in the presence of the Senate and House of Representatives, open all the certificates, and the votes shall then be counted. The person having the greatest number of votes shall be the President, if such number be a majority of the whole number of electors appointed; and if there be more than one who have such majority, and have an equal number of votes, then the House of Representatives shall immediately choose by ballot one of them for President; and if no person have a majority, then from the five highest on the list the said House shall in like manner choose the President. But in choosing the President, the votes shall be taken by States, the representation from each state having one vote; A quorum for this purpose shall consist of a member or members from two thirds of the states, and a majority of all the states shall be necessary to a choice. In every case, after the choice of the President, the person having the greatest number of votes of the electors shall be the Vice President. But if there should remain two or more who have equal votes, the Senate shall choose from them by ballot the Vice President.

The Congress may determine the time of choosing the electors, and the day on which they shall give their votes; which day shall be the same throughout the United States.

No person except a natural born citizen, or a citizen of the United States, at the time of the adoption of this Constitution, shall be eligible to the office of President; neither shall any person be eligible to that office who shall not have attained to the age of thirty five years, and been fourteen Years a resident within the United States.

In case of the removal of the President from office, or of his death, resignation, or inability to discharge the powers and duties of the said office, the same shall devolve on the Vice President, and the Congress may by law provide for the case of removal, death, resignation or inability, both of the President and Vice President, declaring what officer shall then act as President, and such officer shall act accordingly, until the disability be removed, or a President shall be elected.

The President shall, at stated times, receive for his services, a compensation, which shall neither be increased nor diminished during the period for which he shall have been elected, and he shall not receive within that period any other emolument from the United States, or any of them.

Before he enter on the execution of his office, he shall take the following oath or affirmation:—"I do solemnly swear (or affirm) that I will faithfully execute the office of President of the United States, and will to the best of my ability, preserve, protect and defend the Constitution of the United States."

Section 2. The President shall be commander in chief of the Army and Navy of the United States, and of the militia of the several states, when called into the actual service of the United States; he may require the opinion, in writing, of the principal officer in each of the executive departments, upon any subject relating to the duties of their respective offices, and he shall have power to grant reprieves and pardons for offenses against the United States, except in cases of impeachment.

He shall have power, by and with the advice and consent of the Senate, to make treaties, provided two thirds of the Senators present concur; and he shall nominate, and by and with the advice and consent of the Senate, shall appoint ambassadors, other public ministers and consuls, judges of the Supreme Court, and all other officers of the United States, whose appointments are not herein otherwise provided for, and which shall be established by law: but the Congress may by law vest the appointment of such inferior officers, as they think proper, in the President alone, in the courts of law, or in the heads of departments.

The President shall have power to fill up all vacancies that may happen during the recess of the Senate, by granting commissions which shall expire at the end of their next session.

Section 3. He shall from time to time give to the Congress information of the state of the union, and recommend to their consideration such measures as he shall judge necessary and expedient; he may, on extraordinary occasions, convene both Houses, or either of them, and in case of disagreement between them, with respect to the time of adjournment, he may adjourn them to such time as he shall think proper; he shall receive ambassadors and other public ministers; he shall take care that the laws be faithfully executed, and shall commission all the officers of the United States.

Section 4. The President, Vice President and all civil officers of the United States, shall be removed from office on impeachment for, and conviction of, treason, bribery, or other high crimes and misdemeanors.

Article III

Section 1. The judicial power of the United States, shall be vested in one Supreme Court, and in such inferior courts as the Congress may from time to time ordain and establish. The judges, both of the supreme and inferior courts, shall hold their offices during good behaviour, and shall, at stated times, receive for their services, a compensation, which shall not be diminished during their continuance in office.

Section 2. The judicial power shall extend to all cases, in law and equity, arising under this Constitution, the laws of the United States, and treaties made, or which shall be made, under their authority;—to all cases affecting ambassadors, other public ministers and consuls;—to all cases of admiralty and maritime jurisdiction;—to controversies to which the United States shall be a party;—to controversies between two or more states;—between a state and citizens of another state;—between citizens of different states;—between citizens of the same state claiming lands under grants of different states, and between a state, or the citizens thereof, and foreign states, citizens or subjects.

In all cases affecting ambassadors, other public ministers and consuls, and those in which a state shall be party, the Supreme Court shall have original jurisdiction. In all the other cases before mentioned, the Supreme Court shall have appellate jurisdiction, both as to law and fact, with such exceptions, and under such regulations as the Congress shall make.

The trial of all crimes, except in cases of impeachment, shall be by jury; and such trial shall be held in the state where the said crimes shall have been committed; but when not committed within any state, the trial shall be at such place or places as the Congress may by law have directed.

Section 3. Treason against the United States, shall consist only in levying war against them, or in adhering to their enemies, giving them aid and comfort. No person shall be convicted of treason unless on the testimony of two witnesses to the same overt act, or on confession in open court.

The Congress shall have power to declare the punishment of treason, but no attainder of treason shall work corruption of blood, or forfeiture except during the life of the person attainted.

Article IV

Section 1. Full faith and credit shall be given in each state to the public acts, records, and judicial proceedings of every other state. And the Congress may by general laws prescribe the manner in which such acts, records, and proceedings shall be proved, and the effect thereof.

Section 2. The citizens of each state shall be entitled to all privileges and immunities of citizens in the several states.

A person charged in any state with treason, felony, or other crime, who shall flee from justice, and be found in another state, shall on demand of the executive authority of the state from which he fled, be delivered up, to be removed to the state having jurisdiction of the crime.

No person held to service or labor in one state, under the laws thereof, escaping into another, shall, in consequence of any law or regulation therein, be discharged from such service or labor, but shall be delivered up on claim of the party to whom such service or labor may be due.

Section 3. New states may be admitted by the Congress into this union; but no new states shall be formed or erected within the jurisdiction of any other state; nor any state be formed by the junction of two or more states, or parts of states, without the consent of the legislatures of the states concerned as well as of the Congress.

The Congress shall have power to dispose of and make all needful rules and regulations respecting the territory or other property belonging to the United States; and nothing in this Constitution shall be so construed as to prejudice any claims of the United States, or of any particular state.

Section 4. The United States shall guarantee to every state in this union a republican form of government, and shall protect each of them against invasion; and on application of the legislature, or of the executive (when the legislature cannot be convened) against domestic violence.

Article V

The Congress, whenever two thirds of both houses shall deem it necessary, shall propose amendments to this Constitution, or, on the application of the legislatures of two thirds of the several states, shall call a convention for proposing amendments, which, in either case, shall be valid to all intents and purposes, as part of this Constitution, when ratified by the legislatures of three fourths of the several states, or by conventions in three fourths thereof, as the one or the other mode of ratification may be proposed by the Congress; provided that no amendment which may be made prior to the year one thousand eight hundred and eight shall in any manner affect the first and fourth clauses in the ninth section of the first article; and that no state, without its consent, shall be deprived of its equal suffrage in the Senate.

Article VI

All debts contracted and engagements entered into, before the adoption of this Constitution, shall be as valid against the United States under this Constitution, as under the Confederation.

This Constitution, and the laws of the United States which shall be made in pursuance thereof; and all treaties made, or which shall be made, under the authority of the United States, shall be the supreme law of the land; and the judges in every state shall be bound thereby, anything in the Constitution or laws of any State to the contrary notwithstanding.

The Senators and Representatives before mentioned, and the members of the several state legislatures, and all executive and judicial officers, both of the United States and of the several states, shall be bound by oath or affirmation, to support this Constitution; but no religious test shall ever be required as a qualification to any office or public trust under the United States.

Article VII

The ratification of the conventions of nine states, shall be sufficient for the establishment of this Constitution between the states so ratifying the same.

The U.S. Constitution at a Glance	
ARTICLE	**PROVISION**
I	Legislature (House and Senate)
II	Executive (President)
III	Judicial (Supreme Court)
IV	Interstate Relations
V	Amendment Process
VI	National Supremacy
VII	Ratification Process

The road to ratification was not easy. Two groups emerged to argue for and against accepting the Constitution:

- **Federalists: those favoring ratification**
- **Anti-Federalists: those opposing ratification**

A series of articles written by Alexander Hamilton, James Madison, and John Jay entitled *The Federalist Papers* were published under the pseudonym *Publius*. The documents argued the cause for ratification to the American people.

The Anti-Federalists—among them Samuel Adams, Patrick Henry, and Richard Henry Lee—also wrote under a variety of pseudonyms, including Centinel, Brutus, Federal Farmer, and Cato. They argued against the Constitution's ratification. Their primary concern was that the document did not specifically protect individual rights.

In response to the concerns of the Anti-Federalists, the Federalists promised to amend the Constitution to include a Bill of Rights. Based on this promise, the Constitution was ratified in June 1788 and became effective in March 1789.

Amending the Constitution

Amending the Constitution is a two-part process: proposal and ratification. Four formal methods of amendment are defined:

Proposed by:

- **2/3 vote in both houses of Congress**
  - or
- **National convention called by Congress at the request of 2/3 of the states**

Ratified by:

- **Legislatures in 3/4 of the states**
  - or
- **Conventions in 3/4 of the states**

The original Bill of Rights contained twelve amendments, but only ten were passed. The first ten amendments are known as the Bill of Rights. Of the twenty-seven constitutional amendments, all but one, the Twenty-First, have been proposed by two-thirds vote in both houses of Congress and ratified by the legislatures of three-fourths of the states. In the case of the Twenty-First Amendment, repealing Prohibition, the amendment was proposed by two-thirds vote in both houses of Congress and ratified by conventions in three-fourths of the states.

Although no informal method of constitutional change is provided, the Constitution is regarded as a living document and may be interpreted differently over time. This means that the Constitution itself does not change, but rather the way we view the Constitution changes. Processes and outcomes alter the way we interpret the Constitution. One often cited example is the right to privacy. Although no expressed right to privacy exists in the Constitution, the U.S. Supreme Court decision in *Griswold v. Connecticut* (1965) noted "a zone of privacy" implied in the Bill of Rights and the Fourteenth Amendment.

Informative Websites

http://www.constitution.org/afp/afp.htm
Anti-Federalist Papers

http://thomas.loc.gov/home/histdox/fedpapers.html
The Library of Congress: The Federalist Papers

http://www.law.umkc.edu/faculty/projects/ftrials/conlaw/rightofprivacy.html
The Right of Privacy

EXERCISES

EXERCISE 1

Using specific examples from the Constitution, explain how government is structured, what powers are assigned, and how government is limited.

EXERCISE 2

Summarize the arguments in Federalist 10 and 51 from the Library of Congress website (http://thomas.loc.gov/home/histdox/fedpapers.html).

FEDERALISM

Federalism is defined as the constitutional division of power between the national and subnational units of government, in which each unit enforces its laws directly on the people.

Federalism is an important component of the U.S. political system. Though this federal system is constitutionally defined, it is not a static system. The line that divides power between the nation and states has changed over time.

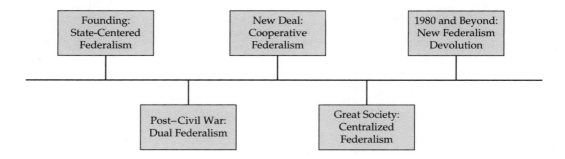

Why Is Federalism Important?

- **Protects liberty**
  - In Federalist 51, James Madison argues, "ambition must be made to counteract ambition" in order to protect liberty, and federalism does so by creating a system of competition among governmental units.

- **Distributes power**
  - By distributing political power broadly among national, state, and local governments, individuals have greater opportunity to participate.

- **Increases participation**
  - More than 1.8 million civil servants

- **Improves efficiency**
  - Allows local governments to respond directly to their citizens in providing immediate services such as police protection, road maintenance, and garbage pickup.

- **Manages conflict**
  - Allows states to solve problems in their own way; reduces conflict at the national level

- **Allows for policy innovation**
  - Distribution of power between the nation and the state allows for experimentation at the lower levels of government. Many national programs, such as Social Security, were initiated at lower levels of government.

- **Responds locally**
  - Government policies administered from afar are often arbitrary, whereas policy made locally is consistent with community needs.

Problems with Federalism

Although the federal system offers many benefits, it also introduces three notable problems:

- **Obstructs action**
  - States retain the authority to act in many areas and argue from the position of states' rights when they find their values in conflict with national issues.
  - *Example:* States that resisted desegregation argued on the basis of states' rights when passing "Jim Crow" laws. Later, despite the ruling in *Brown v. Board of Education* (1954), many of these same states reiterated the argument in an effort to maintain segregated schools. It was not until the passage of the Civil Rights Act of 1964 that the issue of segregation was largely laid to rest.

- **Frustrates national policy**
  - Decentralization or division of power between nation and state can stall work on national projects.
  - *Example:* Local organizations referred to as NIMBYs ("Not in my backyard") have effectively blocked a national program to safely dispose of nuclear waste.

- **Obstruct uniform policy**
  - States administer many social programs with broad guidance from the federal government. As a result, costs and benefits are spread unevenly across the nation.
  - After welfare reform in 1996, states set their own criteria for benefits. A comparison of Temporary Assistance for Needy Families (TANF) benefits in California and Texas reveals that Texas awards less aid to the needy despite the fact that federal tax dollars fund the program.

Temporary Assistance for Needy Families
Aid to Families with Dependent Children

Grants-in-Aid to States

Fiscal federalism can be used to express the relationship between the national government and the states in terms of tax revenues and government expenditures. Transfers of federal funds to lower levels of government are called grants-in-aid to states. The federal grant system is essentially comprised of two types of grants: categorical and block.

Categorical Grants

- Clearly specify how funds are to be spent
- Often have strict provisions attached
- Two types
  - Project Grants (3/4)
    - Awarded on the basis of competitive applications
  - Formula Grants (1/4)
  - Distributed according to a formula that varies depending on the grant
  - States do not have to apply for these grants; rather, the formula dictates the amount of funding each state will receive.

Block Grants

- Adopted in 1966 in response to complaints about the stringent requirements and problems associated with categorical grants
- Allow more flexible spending by states and localities in a variety of areas, including education, public health, and transportation
- Many argue that block grants are more efficient because they allow states to determine how the money should be spent.

Informative Websites

http://www.hud.gov/offices/cpd/communitydevelopment/programs
Community Development Block Grant Program

http://www.ed.gov/fund/grant/about/formgrant.html
U.S. Department of Education: Formula Grants

EXERCISES

EXERCISE 1

Why do you suppose federalism evolves? Identify examples from each period.

EXERCISE 2

Pick one of the problems associated with federalism and explain how it might be remedied.

Policy-Making Institutions

THE EXECUTIVE BRANCH

Article II of the Constitution establishes the executive branch. To qualify to serve as president, Section 1 requires that the candidate be a natural-born citizen at least thirty-five years of age and a resident of the United States for fourteen years prior to taking office.

Constitutional Establishment of the Executive Branch

- *"No person except a natural born Citizen, or a Citizen of the United States, at the time of the Adoption of this Constitution, shall be eligible to the Office of President; neither shall any Person be eligible to that Office who shall not have attained to the Age of thirty-five Years, and been fourteen Years a Resident within the United States."*

Source: The Constitution of the United States Article 2, Section 1, Clause 5

Many rewards and responsibilities befall the individual often considered the leader of the "Free World." In addition to an annual salary of $400,000 that is set by congressional law, additional funds are allocated for expenses and travel, living quarters, health care, transportation, retirement pension, security detail, and an office and staff upon retirement. The responsibilities of the president of the United States are loosely outlined in the Constitution. Five distinct roles include the following:

1. Chief administrator
2. Chief legislator
3. Chief diplomat
4. Chief of state
5. Commander-in-chief

Chief Administrator

The following are the responsibilities of the chief administrator:

- **Implement policy**
- **Supervise the executive branch**
- **Appoint and remove executive officials**
- **Prepare executive budget**

In the role of chief administrator derived from Article II, Section 3—"to take care that the laws be faithfully executed"—the president is responsible for implementing policy. One of the tools used by the president to carry out this role is the issuing of executive orders: formal pronouncements that govern executive branch operations. In addition to implementing policy, as chief administrator the president supervises the executive branch of government, as indicated in Article II, Section 2:

> *The President shall be Commander in Chief of the Army and Navy of the United States, and of the Militia of the several States, when called into the actual Service of the United States; he may require the Opinion, in writing, of the principal Officer in each of the executive Departments, upon any subject relating to the Duties of their respective Offices, and he shall have power to Grant Reprieves and Pardons for Offenses against the United States, except in Cases of Impeachment.*
>
> *Source:* U.S. Constitution, art. II, § 2, cl. 2.

He may also appoint and remove executive officials. Although the power to remove executive officials is not specifically mentioned, it is implied. Grover Cleveland largely won this battle in 1885. Likewise, in this capacity the president prepares the Executive Budget. This is not specified in the Constitution but is required by congressional law in the Budget Accounting Act of 1921. This act requires the president to report on the amount of funding needed in the next fiscal year.

To view a diagram of the executive office of the president, please copy and paste this URL into your Internet browser: http://www.whitehouse.gov/our_government/executive_branch/

Chief Legislator

The following are the responsibilities of the chief legislator:

- **Initiate policy**
- **Veto legislation**
- **Convene a sp ecial session of congress**

As chief legislator the president is responsible for initiating policy under Article II, Section 3. The Constitution requires the president to "give to the Congress information of the State of the Union and recommend to their consideration such measures as he shall judge necessary and expedient." (U.S. Const. art. II, § 3, cl. 1)

This task is challenging during periods of divided government when the president is from one party and Congress is controlled by another. Under conditions such as these you can imagine how difficult it is for the president to get Congress to take up executive-branch policy initiatives. One possible consequence of divided government is gridlock: the inability of government to act decisively on any agenda. However, the president may veto legislation passed by Congress and convene a special session of Congress (U.S. Const. art. II § 3).

Presidential Options When Presented with Legislation	
Sign bill	*Bill becomes law*
Veto bill	*Bill dies unless veto is overridden by 2/3 vote in both houses*
No action	*After 10 days (excluding Sundays): Bill becomes law. Congress adjourns within 10 days: Bill dies (pocket veto).*

Source: Project Vote Smart. *Government 101: How a Bill Becomes Law. Retrieved on May 16, 2009, from http://www.votesmart.org/resource_govt101_02.php#.*

Chief Diplomat

The following are the responsibilities of the chief diplomat:

- **Make treaties**
- **Exercise the power of diplomatic recognition**
- **Make executive agreements**

As chief diplomat, the president makes treaties (U.S. Const. art. II, § 2, cl. 2.). A formal treaty requires the advice and consent of two-thirds of the senators present to ratify it. A prominent example of a treaty that was not ratified was the Treaty of Versailles that formally ended World War I.

As chief diplomat the president also exercises the power of diplomatic recognition. The Constitution states, "He shall receive ambassadors and other public ministers" (U.S. Const. art. II, § 3, cl. 3.). Diplomatic recognition can be defined as a state acknowledging the legitimacy of another state or government. For example, the United States did not recognize the Soviet government until 16 years after the Bolshevik Revolution of 1917 or the Communist government of mainland China until more than 25 years after it took power.

Sometimes the president uses executive agreements, which are agreements between heads of state. Such agreements are embodied in custom and international law, not in the Constitution itself. They have much the same effect as a treaty but do not require Senate approval (U.S. Department of State).

Chief of State

The following are the responsibilities of the chief of state:

- **Represent the nation**
- **Grant reprieves and pardons**
- **Appoint federal Court and Supreme Court judges**

As chief of state, the president represents the nation as its chief of state (U.S. Const. art. 2, § 1, cl. x.).

Commander-in-Chief

The following are the responsibilities of the commander-in-chief:

- **Command U.S. armed forces**
- **Appoint military officers**

In this role, the president is in command of the U.S. armed forces and appoints military officers (U.S. Const. art. II, § 2, cl. 2.). The president can order troops to go anywhere, but Congress has been given the authority to declare war (U.S. Const. art. I, § 8). The president's authority to send troops into harm's way without a formal declaration of war has been controversial at times. For example, in response to President Lyndon B. Johnson's handling of the Vietnam War, Congress passed the War Powers Resolution with the intent of ensuring that Congress had a say in the U.S. involvement in the war. The War Powers Resolution requires the president to do the following:

- **Obtain congressional approval prior to committing U.S. troops to a combat zone**
- **Notify Congress within 48 hours of committing U.S. troops to foreign soil**
- **Withdraw troops within 60 days unless Congress votes to declare war**

Source: War Powers Resolution, 1973

Since that time—and, more important, most recently—Congress generally has authorized the president to use force when sending troops into harm's way. Specifically, P.L. 107-40 and P.L. 107-243 authorized the president to use force in Afghanistan and in Iraq, respectively.

PUBLIC LAW 107–40 107TH CONGRESS

Joint Resolution

To authorize the use of United States Armed Forces against those responsible for the recent attacks launched against the United States.

Whereas, on September 11, 2001, acts of treacherous violence were committed against the United States and its citizens; and

Whereas, such acts render it both necessary and appropriate that the United States exercise its rights to self-defense and to protect United States citizens both at home and abroad; and

Whereas, in light of the threat to the national security and foreign policy of the United States posed by these grave acts of violence; and

Whereas, such acts continue to pose an unusual and extraordinary threat to the national security and foreign policy of the United States; and

Whereas, the President has authority under the Constitution to take action to deter and prevent acts of international terrorism against the United States: Now, therefore, be it

Resolved by the Senate and House of Representatives of the United States of America in Congress assembled,

Section 1. Short Title.

This joint resolution may be cited as the "Authorization for Use of Military Force".

Section 2. Authorization for Use of United States Armed Forces.

a. IN GENERAL.—That the President is authorized to use all necessary and appropriate force against those nations, organizations, or persons he determines planned, authorized, committed, or aided the terrorist attacks that occurred on September 11, 2001, or harbored such organizations or persons, in order to prevent any future acts of international terrorism against the United States by such nations, organizations or persons.

b. WAR POWERS RESOLUTIONS REQUIREMENTS.—

1. **Specific Statutory Authorization.**—Consistent with Section 8(a)(1) of the War Powers Resolution, the Congress declares that this section is intended to constitute specific statutory authorization within the meaning of Section 5(b) of the War Powers Resolution.

2. **Applicability of Other Requirements.**—Nothing in this resolution supercedes any requirement of the War Powers Resolution.

Approved September 18, 2001.

PUBLIC LAW 107–243 107TH CONGRESS

Joint Resolution

To authorize the use of United States Armed Forces against Iraq.

Whereas in 1990 in response to Iraq's war of aggression against and illegal occupation of Kuwait, the United States forged a coalition of nations to liberate Kuwait and its people in order to defend the national security of the United States and enforce United Nations Security Council resolutions relating to Iraq;

Whereas after the liberation of Kuwait in 1991, Iraq entered into a United Nations sponsored cease-fire agreement pursuant to which Iraq unequivocally agreed, among other things, to eliminate its nuclear, biological, and chemical weapons programs and the means to deliver and develop them, and to end its support for international terrorism;

Whereas the efforts of international weapons inspectors, United States intelligence agencies, and Iraqi defectors led to the discovery that Iraq had large stockpiles of chemical weapons and a large scale biological weapons program, and that Iraq had an advanced nuclear weapons development program that was much closer to producing a nuclear weapon than intelligence reporting had previously indicated;

Whereas Iraq, in direct and flagrant violation of the cease-fire, attempted to thwart the efforts of weapons inspectors to identify and destroy Iraq's weapons of mass destruction stockpiles and development capabilities, which finally resulted in the withdrawal of inspectors from Iraq on October 31, 1998;

Whereas in Public Law 105–235 (August 14, 1998), Congress concluded that Iraq's continuing weapons of mass destruction programs threatened vital United States interests and international peace and security, declared Iraq to be in "material and unacceptable breach of its international obligations" and urged the President "to take appropriate action, in accordance with the Constitution and relevant laws of the United States, to bring Iraq into compliance with its international obligations";

Whereas Iraq both poses a continuing threat to the national security of the United States and international peace and security in the Persian Gulf region and remains in material and unacceptable breach of its international obligations by, among other things, continuing to possess and develop a significant chemical and biological weapons capability, actively seeking a nuclear weapons capability, and supporting and harboring terrorist organizations;

Whereas Iraq persists in violating resolution of the United Nations Security Council by continuing to engage in brutal repression of its civilian population thereby threatening international peace and security in the region, by refusing to release, repatriate, or account for non-Iraqi citizens wrongfully detained by Iraq, including an American serviceman, and by failing to return property wrongfully seized by Iraq from Kuwait;

Whereas the current Iraqi regime has demonstrated its capability and willingness to use weapons of mass destruction against other nations and its own people;

Whereas the current Iraqi regime has demonstrated its continuing hostility toward, and willingness to attack, the United States, including by attempting in 1993 to assassinate former President Bush and by firing on many thousands of occasions on United States and Coalition Armed Forces engaged in enforcing the resolutions of the United Nations Security Council;

Whereas members of al Qaida, an organization bearing responsibility for attacks on the United States, its citizens, and interests, including the attacks that occurred on September 11, 2001, are known to be in Iraq;

Whereas Iraq continues to aid and harbor other international terrorist organizations, including organizations that threaten the lives and safety of United States citizens;

Whereas the attacks on the United States of September 11, 2001, underscored the gravity of the threat posed by the acquisition of weapons of mass destruction by international terrorist organizations;

Whereas Iraq's demonstrated capability and willingness to use weapons of mass destruction, the risk that the current Iraqi regime will either employ those weapons to launch a surprise attack against the United States or its Armed Forces or provide them to international terrorists who would do so, and the extreme magnitude of harm that would result to the United States and its citizens from such an attack, combine to justify action by the United States to defend itself;

Whereas United Nations Security Council Resolution 678 (1990) authorizes the use of all necessary means to enforce United Nations Security Council Resolution 660 (1990) and subsequent relevant resolutions and to compel Iraq to cease certain activities that threaten international peace and security, including the development of weapons of mass destruction and refusal or obstruction of United Nations weapons inspections in violation of United Nations Security Council Resolution 687 (1991), repression of its civilian population in violation of United Nations Security Council Resolution 688 (1991), and threatening its neighbors or United Nations operations in Iraq in violation of United Nations Security Council Resolution 949 (1994);

Whereas in the Authorization for Use of Military Force Against Iraq Resolution (Public Law 102–1), Congress has authorized the President "to use United States Armed Forces pursuant to United Nations Security Council Resolution 678 (1990) in order to achieve implementation of Security Council Resolution 660, 661, 662, 664, 665, 666, 667, 669, 670, 674, and 677";

Whereas in December 1991, Congress expressed its sense that it "supports the use of all necessary means to achieve the goals of United Nations Security Council Resolution 687 as being consistent with the Authorization of Use of Military Force Against Iraq Resolution (Public Law 102–1)," that Iraq's repression of its civilian population violates United Nations Security Council Resolution 688 and "constitutes a continuing threat to the peace, security, and stability of the Persian Gulf region," and that Congress, "supports the use of all necessary means to achieve the goals of United Nations Security Council Resolution 688";

Whereas the Iraq Liberation Act of 1998 (Public Law 105–338) expressed the sense of Congress that it should be the policy of the United States to support efforts to remove from power the current Iraqi regime and promote the emergence of a democratic government to replace that regime;

Whereas on September 12, 2002, President Bush committed the United States to "work with the United Nations Security Council to meet our common challenge" posed by Iraq and to "work for the necessary resolutions," while also making clear that "the Security Council resolutions will be enforced, and the just demands of peace and security will be met, or action will be unavoidable";

Whereas the United States is determined to prosecute the war on terrorism and Iraq's ongoing support for international terrorist groups combined with its development of weapons of mass destruction in direct violation of its obligations under the 1991 cease-fire and other United Nations Security Council resolutions make clear that it is in the national security interests of the United States and in furtherance of the war on terrorism that all relevant United Nations Security Council resolutions be enforced, including through the use of force if necessary;

Whereas Congress has taken steps to pursue vigorously the war on terrorism through the provision of authorities and funding requested by the President to take the necessary actions against international terrorists and terrorist organizations, including those nations, organizations, or persons who planned, authorized, committed, or aided the terrorist attacks that occurred on September 11, 2001, or harbored such persons or organizations;

Whereas the President and Congress are determined to continue to take all appropriate actions against international terrorists and terrorist organizations, including those nations, organizations, or persons who planned, authorized, committed, or aided the terrorist attacks that occurred on September 11, 2001, or harbored such persons or organizations;

Whereas the President has authority under the Constitution to take action in order to deter and prevent acts of international terrorism against the United States, as Congress recognized in the joint resolution on Authorization for Use of Military Force (Public Law 107–40); and

Whereas it is in the national security interests of the United States to restore international peace and security to the Persian Gulf region: Now, therefore, be it

Resolved by the Senate and House of Representatives of the United States of America in Congress assembled.

Section 1. Short Title.

This joint resolution may be cited as the "Authorization for Use of Military Force Against Iraq Resolution of 2002".

Section 2. Support for United States Diplomatic Efforts.

The Congress of the United States supports the efforts by the President to—

1. strictly enforce through the United Nations Security Council all relevant Security Council resolutions regarding Iraq and encourages him in those efforts; and

2. obtain prompt and decisive action by the Security Council to ensure that Iraq abandons its strategy of delay, evasion and noncompliance and promptly and strictly complies with all relevant Security Council resolutions regarding Iraq.

Section 3. Authorization for Use of United States Armed Forces.

a. AUTHORIZATION.—The President is authorized to use the Armed Forces of the United States as he determines to be necessary and appropriate in order to—

1. defend the national security of the United States against the continuing threat posed by Iraq; and

2. enforce all relevant United Nations Security Council resolutions regarding Iraq.

b. PRESIDENTIAL DETERMINATION.—In connection with the exercise of the authority granted in subsection (a) to use force the President shall, prior to such exercise or as soon thereafter as may be feasible, but no later than 48 hours after exercising such authority, make available to the Speaker of the House of Representatives and the President pro tempore of the Senate his determination that—

1. reliance by the United States on further diplomatic or other peaceful means alone either (A) will not adequately protect the national security of the United States against the continuing threat posed by Iraq or (B) is not likely to lead to enforcement of all relevant United Nations Security Council resolutions regarding Iraq; and

2. acting pursuant to this joint resolution is consistent with the United States and other countries continuing to take the necessary actions against international terrorist and terrorist organizations, including those nations, organizations, or persons who planned, authorized, committed or aided the terrorist attacks that occurred on September 11, 2001.

c. WAR POWERS RESOLUTION REQUIREMENTS.—

1. Specific Statutory Authorization.—Consistent with Section 8(a)(1) of the War Powers Resolution, the Congress declares that this section is intended to constitute specific statutory authorization within the meaning of Section 5(b) of the War Powers Resolution.

2. Applicaility of Other Requirements.—Nothing in this joint resolution supersedes any requirement of the War Powers Resolution.

Section 4. Reports to Congress.

a. REPORTS.—The President shall, at least once every 60 days, submit to the Congress a report on matters relevant to this joint resolution, including actions taken pursuant to the exercise of authority granted in Section 3 and the status of planning for efforts that are expected to be required after such actions are completed, including those actions described in Section 7 of the Iraq Liberation Act of 1998 (Public Law 105–338).

b. SINGLE CONSOLIDATED REPORT.—To the extent that the submission of any report described in subsection (a) coincides with the submission of any other report on matters relevant to this joint resolution otherwise required to be submitted to Congress pursuant to the reporting requirements of the War Powers Resolution (Public Law 93–148), all such reports may be submitted as a single consolidated report to the Congress.

c. RULE OF CONSTRUCTION.—To the extent that the information required by Section 3 of the Authorization for Use of Military Force Against Iraq Resolution (Public Law 102–1) is included in the report required by this section, such report shall be considered as meeting the requirements of Section 3 of such resolution.

Approved October 16, 2002.

The Twenty-Second Amendment   The Twenty-Second Amendment to the Constitution sets the limit for a president's term of service as two consecutive terms.

The Twenty-Fifth Amendment   The Twenty-Fifth Amendment to the Constitution specifies the order of succession to the presidency should the president be unable to fulfill the position's responsibilities.

Order of Succession to the Presidency

- The Vice President
- Speaker of the House
- President Pro Tempore of the Senate
- Secretary of State
- Secretary of the Treasury
- Secretary of Defense
- Attorney General
- Secretary of the Interior
- Secretary of Agriculture
- Secretary of Commerce
- Secretary of Labor
- Secretary of Health and Human Services
- Secretary of Housing and Urban Development
- Secretary of Transportation
- Secretary of Energy
- Secretary of Education
- Secretary of Veterans Affairs
- Secretary of Homeland Security

Source: Presidential Succession Act of 1947 (3 U.S.C. § 19)

Informative Websites

http://www.usconstitution.net
U.S. Constitution Online

http://www.whitehouse.gov
U.S. White House

Bibliography

Almanac of Policy Issues. *War Powers Resolution of 1973*. Retrieved on May 17, 2009, from http://www.policyalmanac.org/world/archive/war_powers_resolution.shtml.

Project Vote Smart. *GOVERNMENT 101: How a Bill Becomes* Law. Retrieved on May 16, 2009, from http://www.votesmart.org/resource_govt101_02.php#.

U.S. Department of State. *Treaty vs. Executive Agreement*. Retrieved on May 16, 2009, from http://www.state.gov/s/l/treaty/faqs/70133.htm.

EXERCISE 1

List and explain the five roles of the president.

EXERCISE 2

If the president were unable to carry out his duties, explain what governmental actions would occur and who would be responsible for oversight.

THE LEGISLATIVE BRANCH

The legislative branch was established by Article I of the U.S. Constitution. It provides for a Congress that is bicameral—that is, two houses composed of the House of Representatives apportioned by population and a Senate composed of two members per state.

Both the House and the Senate have concurrent powers, meaning equal responsibility for declaring war, maintaining armed forces, and so on (U.S. Const. art. I, § 8). Each Congress since the first is ordered numerically. For example, the Congress that meets from 2009 to the end of 2010 will be the 111th Congress. Congress convenes pursuant to Section 2 of the Twentieth Amendment and has two sessions.

| Requirements for Members of Congress ||
HOUSE OF REPRESENTATIVES	SENATE
At least 25 years old	At least 30 years old
U.S. citizen for the past 7 years	U.S. citizen for the past 9 years
Live in the state they represent	Live in the state they represent

Source: U.S. Const, art. 1, § 2, cl. 2, and art. 3, § 3, cl. 3.

House of Representatives

The House of Representatives has 435 members. This number is set by congressional law and is set following reapportionment after the census as directed by the Constitution (art. I, § 2, cl. 3). Each member serves a term of 2 years, and elections are held at the end of each term in the even-numbered years. The members serve their congressional districts. Congressional districts are drawn by the various state legislatures. The unique powers granted to the House of Representatives by the Constitution include originating tax bills and bringing charges of impeachment (art. I, § 82, cl. 4 & 5).

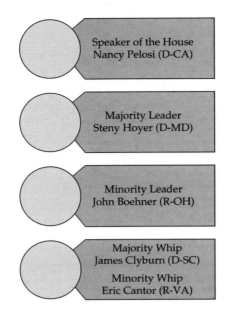

The House of Representatives has a well-defined leadership structure. The political party that controls Congress occupies the leadership roles.

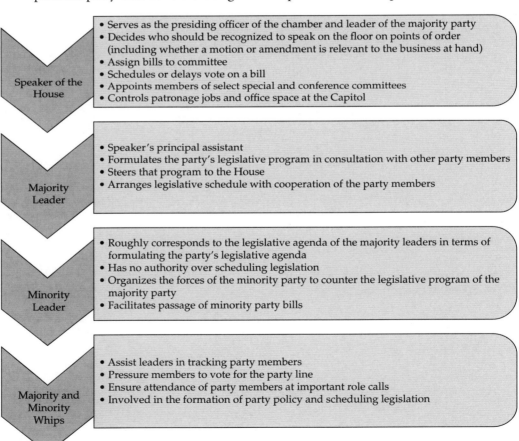

Speaker of the House
- Serves as the presiding officer of the chamber and leader of the majority party
- Decides who should be recognized to speak on the floor on points of order (including whether a motion or amendment is relevant to the business at hand)
- Assign bills to committee
- Schedules or delays vote on a bill
- Appoints members of select special and conference committees
- Controls patronage jobs and office space at the Capitol

Majority Leader
- Speaker's principal assistant
- Formulates the party's legislative program in consultation with other party members
- Steers that program to the House
- Arranges legislative schedule with cooperation of the party members

Minority Leader
- Roughly corresponds to the legislative agenda of the majority leaders in terms of formulating the party's legislative agenda
- Has no authority over scheduling legislation
- Organizes the forces of the minority party to counter the legislative program of the majority party
- Facilitates passage of minority party bills

Majority and Minority Whips
- Assist leaders in tracking party members
- Pressure members to vote for the party line
- Ensure attendance of party members at important role calls
- Involved in the formation of party policy and scheduling legislation

Senate

In the Senate, members serve a 6-year term. There are 100 members, two representing each state. To ensure that this remains the more stable body in Congress, elections are held for one-third of the members every two years (U.S. Const. art. I, § 3, cl. 2.) The constituents of senators are the citizens of the states that elect them.

Unique powers of the Senate include the authority to advise and consent on the ratification of treaties and the confirmation of presidential appointments by two-thirds vote of the members present (U.S. Const. art. II, § 2, cl. 2) and to try impeachment charges (U.S. Const. art. I, § 3, cl. 6). The Senate has a well-structured leadership.

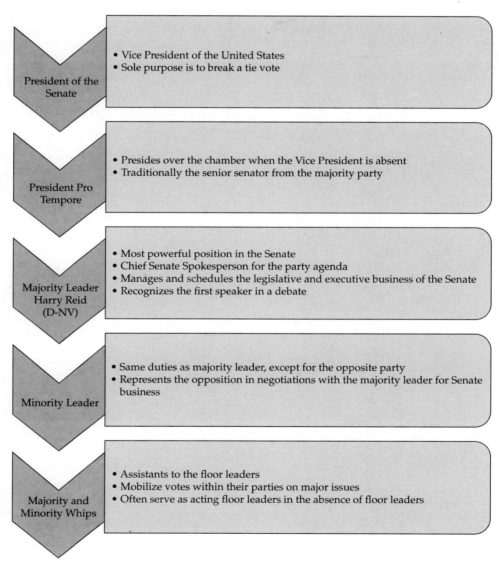

President of the Senate
- Vice President of the United States
- Sole purpose is to break a tie vote

President Pro Tempore
- Presides over the chamber when the Vice President is absent
- Traditionally the senior senator from the majority party

Majority Leader Harry Reid (D-NV)
- Most powerful position in the Senate
- Chief Senate Spokesperson for the party agenda
- Manages and schedules the legislative and executive business of the Senate
- Recognizes the first speaker in a debate

Minority Leader
- Same duties as majority leader, except for the opposite party
- Represents the opposition in negotiations with the majority leader for Senate business

Majority and Minority Whips
- Assistants to the floor leaders
- Mobilize votes within their parties on major issues
- Often serve as acting floor leaders in the absence of floor leaders

Source: U.S. Const. art. I, § 3, cl. 4; art. II, § 2, cl. 2; and art. I, § 3, cl. 6.

How Bills Get Passed

To understand how bills are passed into law, it is important to understand the committee system. The committee system of the U.S. Congress encourages member specialization in particular areas. Members seek to be appointed to various committees because of their policy interests, media attention, and relative importance.

Of the up to 15,000 bills introduced each session, less than 10 percent are passed (Singer, 2008), and most bills die in committee.

Committees

- **House:** Elected within 7 days of Congress convening
- **Senate:** Appointed by resolution at the beginning of each Congress with power to continue to act until the successors are appointed
- **Both House and Senate**
  - Members are in proportion to the seats held by the parties in Congress
  - Chaired by a member of the majority party
  - Most of the real work on legislation goes on in committees.
  - Principal function of the committee is the screening and drafting of legislation.

Senate Standing Committees

- Agriculture, Nutrition & Forestry
- Appropriations
- Armed Services
- Banking, Housing & Urban Affairs
- Budget
- Commerce, Science & Transportation
- Energy and Natural Resources
- Environment and Public Works
- Finance
- Foreign Relations
- Health, Education, Labor & Pensions
- Homeland Security and Governmental Affairs
- Judiciary
- Rules and Administration
- Small Business and Entrepreneurship
- Veterans Affairs

Source: United States Senate. *Committees.* Retrieved on May 15, 2009, from http://www.senate.gov/pagelayout/committees/d_three_sections_with_teasers/committees_home.htm

House of Representatives Standing Committees

- Agriculture
- Appropriations
- Armed Services
- Budget
- Education & Labor
- Energy & Commerce
- Financial Services
- Foreign Affairs
- Homeland Security
- House Administration
- Judiciary
- Natural Resources
- Oversight & Government Reform
- Rules
- Science & Technology
- Small Business
- Standards of Official Conduct
- Transportation & Infrastructure
- Veterans Affairs
- Ways & Means

Source: U.S. Government Printing Office. *Congressional Committee Materials Online via GPO* Access. Retrieved on May 16, 2009, from http://www.gpoaccess.gov/congress/index.html

The following is the typical route a proposed bill follows to passage as law:

1. Bill is introduced and assigned a number.
2. Bill is assigned to a standing committee.
3. Bill is referred to a subcommittee.
   a. Subunit of the standing committee
4. In subcommittee, hearings are held and testimony is provided.
   a. Testimony is often provided by experts who are interest-group lobbyists.
   b. By refusing to hold hearings, the subcommittee can effectively condemn the bill.
5. After hearings are completed, the bill is marked up.
   a. Line-by-line revision or editing of the legislation
6. If the bill is approved, it goes back to full committee.

7. If approved by full committee, the bill is reported to the full House and placed on the House calendar.

    a. Bills are not placed on the calendar in chronological order, and many die here without ever reaching the floor.

8. To reach the House floor, a bill must receive a rule from the Rules Committee.

    a. A rule governs the bill's consideration on the floor, how long it can be debated, whether it can be amended, and so on.

    b. The Rules Committee can kill a bill simply by refusing to give it a rule.

9. If the bill receives a rule from the Rules Committee, it goes to the full House for debate amendment and ultimate passage.

10. If the House version is different from the Senate version, the versions must go to a conference committee.

    a. Conference committees are composed of both House members and Senators who meet to reconcile differences between the bills.

    b. Upon agreement, a compromise bill is sent back to both the House and Senate for passage.

11. If the bill passes the House and the Senate, it is then presented to the president for signature.

Informative Websites

http://www.votesmart.org/resource_govt101_02.php#
Project Vote Smart: How a Bill Becomes Law

www.house.gov
U.S. House of Representatives

www.senate.gov
U.S. Senate

Bibliography

Singer, Paul. Members Offered Many Bills but Passed Few. *Roll Call.* Retrieved on May 16, 2009, from http://www.rollcall.com/issues/54_61/news/30466-1.html.

U.S. Government Printing Office. *Congressional Committee Materials Online via GPO* Access. Retrieved on May 16, 2009, from http://www.gpoaccess.gov/congress/index.html.

U.S. Senate. *Committees.* Retrieved on May 15, 2009, from http://www.senate.gov/pagelayout/committees/d_three_sections_with_teasers/committees_home.htm.

EXERCISES

EXERCISE 1

Create a chart that identifies members of both the House and Senate by ethnicity and gender.

EXERCISE 2

Identify the individuals holding current leadership roles in both the House and Senate, and explain what they do.

THE JUDICIAL BRANCH

The judicial branch consists of a three-tiered federal court system. The Constitution in Article III created the judicial branch and established one Supreme Court, but the statement "and in such inferior Courts as the Congress may from time to time ordain and establish" allowed for the creation of additional courts (U.S. Const. art. III, § 1, cl. 1). This was done almost immediately with the Judiciary Act of 1789. The three-tiered federal court system is composed of the following:

- **Supreme Court at the highest level**
- **United States Courts of Appeal at the middle level**
- **United States District Courts at the lowest level**

The courts have two types of jurisdiction:

> **Original Jurisdiction:** the authority to hear a case for the first time
>
> **Appellate Jurisdiction:** the authority to review the records of the trial court and oral or written arguments or briefs submitted by attorneys

United States District Courts	United States Courts of Appeals	The United States Supreme Court

- Original jurisdiction over cases involving:
  - Federal crimes
  - Civil lawsuits under federal law
  - Civil cases between citizens in amounts greater than $50,000
  - Admiralty and maritime cases
  - Bankruptcy cases
  - The review of certain actions of federal administrative agencies
  - Others matters assigned to them by Congress
	- Appellate jurisdiction only
	  - Do not hold trials or accept new evidence
	- Hear cases on appeals from
	  - Federal District Courts
	  - U.S. regulatory commissions
	  - Certain other federal courts
		- Original jurisdiction over cases involving:
		  - Two or more states
		  - The federal district and a state
		  - Foreign ambassadors and other diplomats
		  - A state and a citizen of a different state if initiated by the state
		- Appelate juridiction at its own discretion
		- Generally follows the rule of four: if at least four of the nine justices want hear a case on appeal, the court call up the lower court record by issuing a writ of certiorari

U.S. District Courts

- **District courts are named for geographic regions of the state:**
  - *Example:* San Marcos, Texas, is within the jurisdiction of the U.S. District Court for the Western District of Texas.
- **District courts are presided over by federal district judges who are appointed for life by the president and confirmed by the Senate.**
- **Approximately 94 district courts are located throughout the United States.**

To view photos of the District Court, please visit http://www.uscourts.gov/districtcourts.html

U.S. Courts of Appeals

- **Courts of appeals are also known as federal circuit courts.**
- **Courts of appeals have only appellate jurisdiction.**
- **Twelve courts of appeals, plus the Federal Circuit Court in Washington, DC, are organized by region:**
  - *Example:* Texas, Louisiana, and Mississippi constitute the 5th Circuit Court.

To view a circuit court map, please visit http://www.uscourts.gov/courtlinks/

U.S. Supreme Court

The U.S. Supreme Court is provided for in the Constitution, Article III: "the judicial power of the United States, shall be vested in one supreme Court." This court is organized as follows:

- **Has both original and appellate jurisdiction (art. III, § 1).**
- **Is the final interpreter on all matters involving:**
  - The Constitution
  - Federal laws and treaties
  - Appeals from lower courts
- **Each of the nine members is appointed for life by the President of the United States and confirmed by the Senate.**
- **The Chief Justices are appointed by the president and are subject to Senate approval.**

To view photos of the current Supreme Court, please visit http://www.supremecourtus.gov/

Judicial Restraint versus Judicial Activism

Two judicial positions affect law and policy: the position of judicial restraint and the position of judicial activism.

President of Judicial Restraint

- View the judiciary as the least democratic branch of government
- Rely on original intent when interpreting the law and the Constitution
- Prestrict constructionists

President of Judicial Activism

- View the Constitution as a living document
- Reshape Constitutional meaning to fit the needs of contemporary society
- Vigorously review the actions of other branches of government
- In a sense, interpret new meaning into the Constitution

One thing is clear, whether you subscribe to the position of restraint or activism: Justices, in their capacity to rule on all matters involving law and the Constitution, are policymakers.

Access to the Courts

One does not have access to the court unless one has standing. Standing is the legal right to initiate a lawsuit. To do so, a person must be sufficiently affected by the matter at hand, and it must be possible to resolve a case or controversy by legal action ('Lectric Law Library). At times, one's wealth as well as the influence of interest groups have influenced judicial access and decisions.

Informative Websites

http://www.uscourts.gov
U.S. Courts: The Federal Judicial System

Bibliography

Federal Judicial Center. *History of the Federal Judiciary.* Retrieved on July 8, 2009, from http://www.fjc.gov/history/home.nsf.

The 'Lectric Law Library. *Legal Definition of Standing.* Retrieved on May 16, 2009, from http://www.lectlaw.com/def2/s064.htm.

EXERCISES

EXERCISE 1

List and explain the jurisdiction of each of the courts.

EXERCISE 2

Identify and discuss three differences between judicial restraint and judicial activism.

AMERICAN POLITICAL CULTURE

Political culture is a key component in sustaining and legitimizing the U.S. government. It can be defined as follows:

A shared body of values and beliefs that shapes perceptions and attitudes toward politics and government and in turn influences political behavior.

Common Values	
Rights of Citizenship	Voting First Amendment Rights
Obligations of Citizenship	Obeying the Law
Rules for Participation	Who May Vote Requirements for Holding Office

↓

**Legitimacy
Sustenance**

The fact that citizens agree on these values means that they tend to perceive the government as legitimate, and thereby worth sustaining. Unlike other countries in the world, such as Pakistan, the American political system, its Constitution, and the institutions and processes through which they operate are relatively stable. Can you imagine the alternative? Perhaps government would be ineffective, or perhaps in order to act it would force us to comply.

Ironically, our relatively stable system and our common political culture do not mean that we take full advantage of participating in the system. Here are some interesting average statistics:

- **About 50 percent voter turnout in presidential elections**
- **Less than 40 percent voter turnout in congressional elections**
- **About 30 percent do nothing**

Source: U.S. Census Bureau, 2008

How Do We Form Our Political Beliefs?

Our beliefs are closely linked to our opinions. We derive these beliefs and opinions through a process of socialization. Primary modes of socialization include these:

- **Family**
- **Schools**
- **Churches**
- **Peers**
- **Media**

The media is one of the most important sources of socialization for politics. It is important because the news—in whatever form—is delivered as a story, within a context, with a meaning assigned, and with possible outcomes considered.

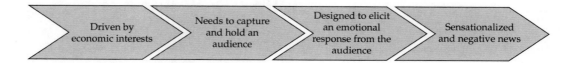

In one survey, over 90 percent of those sampled derived their information about current affairs, including politics and government, from some media source (Pew Research Center, 2007), including newspapers, television, and the Internet. Among these sources, television was the most influential source.

The media is driven by economic interests because of its need to capture and hold an audience. Because of this, visual media and, to some degree, print media are designed to elicit an emotional response from the audience. As a result, much of what we see or read is sensationalized and often tends toward negativism.

The media has long considered itself the watchdog of the public trust, meaning that it is the media's perceived role to uncover corruption and wrongdoing. Much of our information comes from the media, and the media essentially has the capacity to set the agenda. This means that the media controls the message, which is what we talk about or perceive as important. If we perceive an issue as important, then we will talk about it. If the issue gains salience, then legislatures will act.

Some believe that the media expresses a liberal bias that favors the Democratic agenda. In fact, in the effort to secure an audience, media caters to all ideological positions.

Informative Websites

http://www.people-press.org
Pew Research Center

http://www.census.gov
U.S. Census Bureau

Bibliography

Pew Research Center for the People & the Press. (2007, April). *Public Knowledge of Current Affairs Little Changed by News and Information Revolutions: What Americans Know: 1989–2007*. Retrieved on May 16, 2009, from http://people-press.org/report/319/public-knowledge-of-current-affairs-little-changed-by-news-and-information-revolutions.

U.S. Census Bureau. (2008, June). *Voting and Registration in the Election of November 2006*. Retrieved on May 16, 2009, from http://www.census.gov/population/www/socdemo/voting.html.

EXERCISE 1

List the shared values of American political culture, and give an example of each.

EXERCISE 2

Explain five ways the media influences our political beliefs.

POLITICAL PARTIES AND INTEREST GROUPS

Two-Party System

The United States has a two-party system for several reason:

- **Cultural consensus**
- **Electoral rules**
- **Restrictions on minor parties**

Cultural Consensus

Some historical precedents, combined with core values and central policy tendencies, serve to sustain the U.S. two-party system:

- **Core values**
- **Central policy**
  - A tendency to cluster around the center of most policy issues
- **Historical precedents**
  - Concept of a two-party system has been reinforced and has gained acceptance through custom.
  - The nation's first party system developed from two coalitions: the Federalists and the anti-Federalists (National Endowment for the Humanities).

Electoral Rules

The methods employed for selecting representatives—winner-take-all and proportional representation—serve to maintain a two-party system and disadvantage minor parties.

Winner-Take-All

- U.S. system
- Single-member districts
- Each district elects one person to office on the basis of who won the most votes.
- Discourages minority or third-party efforts
- From the voter's point of view, a vote for a minor party is wasted.

Source: Office of the Federal Register. *U.S. Electoral College FAQ.* Retrieved on May 16, 2009, from http://www.archives.gov/federal-register/electoral-college/faq.html.

Proportional Representation

- Most other democratic nations, including Germany, Austria, Canada, and France
- Legislative seats are apportioned to political parties in proportion to the popular vote that each party receives.
- From the voter's point of view, in this system a vote for the minor party is not wasted.

Source: World Policy Institute. *What Is Proportional Representation?* Retrieved on May 16, 2009, from http://www.worldpolicy.org/projects/globalrights/democracy/abcs-html.

Restrictions on Minor Parties

- **Ballot Access**
  - Whereas Democratic and Republican candidates are automatically placed on ballots, minor parties and independents must meet various requirements in each state.
  - A common requirement might be to obtain a petition signed by a percentage of registered voters and then win a percentage of the vote in any given election to remain on subsequent ballots.

- **Public Funding**
  - In presidential election campaigns, only partial federal funds are given to minor parties to run their conventions based on their candidates' share of the popular vote in the preceding presidential election.
  - Federal matching of funds for campaigns requires that the candidate receive 5 percent of the vote in the general election to be eligible (Federal Elections Commission, 2009)

Texas Ballot Access

- For a new party candidate to be placed on the ballot for statewide office in Texas, the candidate must have the support of 43,992 qualified voters.
- If the candidate receives a majority of the votes cast at the county, district, or state convention, the name will be placed on the ballot for the general election.

Source: Texas Secretary of State. *New Party Nominees or Parties Without Ballot Access.* Retrieved on May 16, 2009, from http://www.sos.state.tx.us/elections/candidates/guide/newparty.shtml.

Political Parties   Political parties are intermediary organizations that operate between the electorate and government with the goal of getting their members elected to office.

Typology of Parties

Party in the electorate	Any individual who claims party affiliation
Party in the government	Elected officials and the party they represent
Party as an organization	Structure of the organization itself, including precinct chairs, county chairs, state committee members, etc. Links the party and the electorate to the party and government

Source: Key, V. O. (1942). *Politics, parties, and pressure groups.* New York: Thomas Y. Crowell Company.

There are many types of minor parties:

- **Ideological parties**
  - Exist to promote an ideology (a system of ideas and ideals)

○ *Example:* Libertarians

- **Protest parties**
  ○ Arise around popular issues or concerns that major parties have failed to address
  ○ *Example:* Populist party of the late 1800s arose as a protest by farmers against eastern railroad monopolies on the gold standard.

- **Single-issue parties**
  ○ Form around a particular cause
  ○ Similar to protest parties but much narrower in policy focus
  ○ *Example:* Green party focuses on environmental protection

- **Splinter parties**
  ○ Formed by a dissatisfied faction of a major party
  ○ *Example:* Dixiecrats in 1948 split from the Democratic Party because of their platform on civil rights.

A Responsible Party Model   In the ideal world, a party would adopt a platform that does the following:

- **Sets forth its principles and policy positions**
- **Recruits candidates from among its members who agree with the party's platform**
- **Informs and educates the public on the party's platform**
- **Organizes and directs campaigns based on the platform principles**
- **Organizes the legislature to ensure party control in policy making**
- **Makes all of its elected officials accountable for enacting the party's platform**

However, this model is not truly applicable under today's conditions. Several key points emerge:

- **Winning wins over principle: To garner a majority of the vote, there is no incentive to take strong policy positions.**
- **Campaigns are not managed by the parties but by professional organizations.**
- **Candidates are not recruited by their parties but rather by primary elections.**
- **No formal method is in place to bind elected officials to the party platform once they have been elected.**

http://spot.colorado.edu/~mcguire/rptheo.html

Interest Groups   Interest groups are intermediary organizations composed of individuals with a common interest. They provide the basis for the individuals' actions in relation to government, with the goal of influencing governmental policy.

Interest groups form for a variety of reasons:

- **To protect their economic interests**
  ○ *Example:* Business organizations

- **To advance social movements**
  - *Example:* National Association for the Advancement of Colored People (NAACP) for the Civil Rights Movement
- **To seek government benefits**
  - *Example:*
- **To request or respond to government regulation**
  - *Example:* Sierra Club

As government expands, interest groups form to secure their portion of government benefits.

Business and Trade Organization	• Most numerous • *Example:* Business roundtable
Professional Organizations	• *Example:* American Medical Association, American Bar Association
Labor Organizations	• *Example:* AFL-CIO
Farm Organizations	• *Example:* National Grange
Specialized Groups	• *Example:* Milk producers
Women's Organizations	• *Example:* National Organization for Women
Religious Groups	• *Example:* Christian Coalition, American Israeli Public Affairs Committee
Public Interest Groups	• Those that represent or claim to represent the broader base of American society • *Example:* Common Cause—originally formed to promote governmental regulation in areas of consumer safety, now encompasses a wide variety of causes including election law reform and public financing of elections
Single-Issue Groups	• Appeal to a particular principle or belief • *Example:* National Abortion and Reproductive Rights Action League • Oftentimes the creation of one group spurs the creation of a group on the other side of the exact same issue, such as the National Right to Life Organization that opposes pro-choice.
Ideological Groups	• Pursue the liberal or conservative agendas • *Example:* Americans for Democratic Action, American Conservative Union
Government Lobbies	• At the state and local level • *Example:* National Governors Association, National League of Cities, Association of Counties

How Do Interest Groups Operate?   Interest groups utilize both direct and indirect lobbying:

- **Direct lobbying tactics**
  - Public relations
    - Efforts to promote interests not only in government but in the public mainstream by advertising, etc.
  - Access to government officials
  - Information
    - Many lobbyists are often insiders or ex-legislators.
    - Once a lobbyist gains access, his or her expertise and knowledge become invaluable sources to those they lobby.
    - Lobbyists fully understand the legislative process, track bills, and know what committees and subcommittees are working on that are relevant to their interests.
    - Lobbyists often testify as experts at subcommittee hearings.

- **Indirect lobbying**
  - Grassroots mobilization
    - Efforts to mobilize the constituents of a legislator to write letters and make calls about an important issue or to mobilize the constituents to vote for or against certain candidates based on their policy stance
    - Has the effect of molding public opinion
    - *Example:* American Association of Retired Persons (AARP) has been extremely successful in this area.
  - Coalition building
    - Interest groups seek to form coalitions with similarly minded interest groups in order to strengthen their position on a specific piece of legislation.
    - *Example:* It might not be uncommon to find the National Organization of Women (NOW), the League of Women Voters (LWV), and the National Abortion and Reproductive Rights Action League (NARAL) acting in concert on women's issues.

Rarely do individuals engage directly in interest-group tactics. However, individual participation could include acting in protests or demonstrations designed to show disapproval. A notable example of protests are those arising around the World Trade Organization meetings (Yale Center for the Study of Globalization, 2003). Another form of direct involvement is civil disobedience: peaceful but illegal protest activity in which participants knowingly violate the law and allow themselves to be arrested and punished. The best example of this type of activity are the actions of such individuals as Rosa Parks during the Civil Rights Movement.

Informative Websites

http://www.fec.gov
  Federal Elections Commission

http://www.democrats.org/
  The Democratic Party

http://www.rnc.org/splashpage/index.aspx
  National Republican Committee

Bibliography

Common Cause. *About Us.* Retrieved on May 16, 2009, from http://www.commoncause.org/site/pp.asp?c=dkLNK1MQIwG&b=4764181.

Federal Elections Commission. (2009, January). *Public Funding of Presidential Elections Brochure.* Retrieved on May 16, 2009, from http://www.fec.gov/pages/brochures/pubfund.shtml#Primary.

Key, V. O. (1942) *Politics, parties, and pressure groups.* New York, Thomas Y. Crowell Company.

National Endowment for the Humanities. *The First American Party System: Federalists and Democratic-Republicans: The Platforms They Never Had.* Retrieved on May 16, 2009, from http://edsitement.neh.gov/view_lesson_plan.asp?id=560.

Office of the Federal Register. *U.S. Electoral College FAQ.* Retrieved on May 16, 2009, from http://www.archives.gov/federal-register/electoral-college/faq.html.

Texas Secretary of State. *New Party Nominees or Parties Without Ballot Access.* Retrieved on May 16, 2009, from http://www.sos.state.tx.us/elections/candidates/guide/newparty.shtml.

World Policy Institute. *What Is Proportional Representation?* Retrieved on May 16, 2009, from http://www.worldpolicy.org/projects/globalrights/democracy/abcs.html.

Yale Center for the Study of Globalization. (2003, September). *Protests Greet Yet Another WTO Meeting.* Retrieved on May 16, 2009, from http://yaleglobal.yale.edu/display.article?id=2390.

EXERCISE 1

Give examples of five types of interest groups, and identify their goals.

EXERCISE 2

List two examples of direct and indirect lobbying techniques.

VOTING AND ELECTIONS

When the United States was young, voting was restricted. Early limits on voting rights included requirements pertaining to three matters:

- **Property**
- **Religion**
- **Gender**

Essentially, those who voted were white Protestant men who owned property. After the Civil War and the passage of the Thirteenth, Fourteenth, and Fifteenth Amendments, "right of citizens of the United States to vote shall not be denied or abridged by the United States or by any state on account of race, color, or previous condition of servitude" (U.S. Const. amend. XV), many dissatisfied states passed laws designed to affect Black Americans.

Disenfranchisement Techniques		
	WHAT WAS IT?	**WHEN WAS IT ABOLISHED?**
Literacy tests	Tests were administered by clerks at local polling places and rarely administered to illiterate whites	National elections: Voting Rights Act of 1965 State elections: Voting Rights Act amendments of 1970
Grandfather clause	Exempted those whose grandfathers had the right to vote before 1867, before any blacks had the right to vote in the South	1915 in the Supreme Court case Guinn v. United States
Poll taxes	A tax or fee charged at the polls before one could vote	National elections: 1964 by the Twenty-Fourth Amendment State elections: 1966
White primaries	Blacks were barred from voting in primary elections in which party nominees were chosen	1944 in the Supreme Court case Smith v. Allwright

During the progressive reforms of the late nineteenth century a period of high-minded activism, efforts were made to correct social ills, including the powers wielded by political party machines (*Columbia Encyclopedia*, 2007). These reforms included the following:

- **Choosing candidates by primary election**
- **Change in voter registry laws in which registering to vote became the responsibility of the individual**

- **Use of nonpartisan ballots**
- **Use of secret ballots**

The problem with changing voter registry laws is that it takes time and effort for the individual to register to vote. In fact, voting has declined as the right to vote has been expanded by the Fifteenth Nineteenth, and Twenty-Sixth Amendments.

Fifteenth Amendment	Nineteenth Amendment	Twenty-Sixth Amendment
• "Right of citizens of the United States to vote shall not be denied or abridged by the United States or by any state on account of race, color, or previous condition of servitude."	• "The right of citizens of the United States to vote shall not be denied or abridged by the United States or by any State on account of sex."	• "The right of citizens of the United States, who are eighteen years of age or older, to vote shall not be denied or abridged by the United States or by any State on account of age"

Why Don't People Vote?

Satisfaction	• Population satisfied with the way government is conducting policy
Turned Off	• Too much negativism in campaigning • Feeling as though vote doesn't count
Social Mobility	• United States is a highly mobile society, and we vote with our feet by moving to another location. • People have to re-register to vote every time they move.
Barriers to Registration	• Registering is time-consuming.
Failure of Parties	• Political parties do not articulate the party's policy positions, clearly making it difficult for individuals to find information, and thereby make an informed choice.
Rational Calculation	• Locating your polling place, standing in line, and casting your vote might be too costly for those who depend on hourly wages for a living.

Nevertheless, presidential elections bring out the highest number of voters. This is ironic because individuals have less influence at the highest level of national office than they would if they decided to vote in a local election in which their influence is much greater.

Electing a President: The Electoral College

Article II of the Constitution specifies that the president of the United States is to be selected by the Electoral College.

> *The Electors shall meet in their respective States, and vote by Ballot for two persons, of whom one at least shall not lie an Inhabitant of the same State with themselves. And they shall make a List of all the Persons voted for, and of the Number of Votes for each; which List they shall sign and certify, and transmit sealed to the Seat of the Government of the United States, directed to the President of the Senate. The President of the Senate shall, in the Presence of the Senate and House of Representatives, open all the Certificates, and the Votes shall then be counted. The Person having the greatest Number of Votes shall be the President, if such Number be a Majority of the whole Number of Electors appointed; and if there be more than one who have such Majority, and have an equal Number of Votes, then the House of Representatives shall immediately chuse by Ballot one of them for President; and if no Person have a Majority, then from the five highest on the List the said House shall in like Manner chuse the President. But in chusing the President, the Votes shall be taken by States, the Representation from each State having one Vote; a quorum for this Purpose shall consist of a Member or Members from two-thirds of the States, and a Majority of all the States shall be necessary to a Choice. In every Case, after the Choice of the President, the Person having the greatest Number of Votes of the Electors shall be the Vice President. But if there should remain two or more who have equal Votes, the Senate shall choose from them by Ballot the Vice-President.*

Source: U.S. Const. art. II, § 1, cl. 3.

Although this is the official method of selecting the U.S. president, the process is practiced differently today. Today, the process unfolds as follows:

- **Political parties in each state nominate—by convention, committee, or other method—groups of presidential electors.**
  - Equal to the number of representatives each state has in Congress.

- **On Election Day (first Tuesday after the first Monday in November), voters cast ballots for presidential electors. The electors with the most votes win.**
  - The names of the electors are not on the ballot; instead the names of the party candidates are seen.

- **In each state on the first Monday after the second Wednesday in December, the electors meet in the state capitol to cast their vote for president.**
  - The Constitution states that electors are free agents, meaning they can vote for whomever they choose, but they are pledged to their party.

- **Votes are totaled on January 6 in front of the House and Senate, and whoever wins (receives 270 of the 538 total electoral votes) is elected.**

Problems have occurred in the past with this process. The Constitution states that if no clear majority for president is obtained, the president is selected in the House of Representatives. This was the case twice:

- **Thomas Jefferson in 1800**
- **John Quincy Adams in 1824**

On four occasions, candidates who did not receive the popular vote (the most votes cast among the national population) became president because they did receive the requisite electoral votes:

- **John Quincy Adams in 1824**
- **Rutherford B. Hayes in 1876**
- **William Henry Harrison in 1888**
- **George W. Bush in 2000**

The populous does not elect the president. As devised, the electoral system favors large states because of the winner-take-all system. The question is, should we scrap the Electoral College? Some would argue that we should because the system violates the principle of one person/one vote: A vote in a heavily populated state weighs more than a vote cast in a sparsely populated state. On the other hand, no federal mechanism is in place for voting: Voting is controlled by the individual states with the responsibility falling to the individual secretaries secretary of state. In recent history an opportunity to change the process occurred after the hotly contested Bush–Gore 2000 election; however, the tragedy of September 11, 2001, redirected our focus.

Informative websites

http://www.sos.state.tx.us/elections/candidates/guide/newparty.shtml
Texas Secretary of State

http://projectvote.org/?gclid=COqR3Ij00JsCFRdGxwodemSing
Project Vote

Bibliography

Columbia Encyclopedia, 6th ed. Progressivism. (2007). In. Retrieved on May 16, 2009, from http://www.bartleby.com/65/pr/progrsvsm.html.

EXERCISE 1

Identify the advantages and disadvantages of the electoral process.

EXERCISE 2

List and explain five possible reasons for low voter turnout.

Texas Politics

TEXAS HISTORY

The flags of six nations—Spain, France, Mexico, Republic of Texas, Confederate States of America, and the United States of America—have flown over Texas. In order to understand Texas politics, it is helpful to explore the state's rich and diverse history.

Cultural History

Texas is one of the largest states in the United States and consists of a variety of regions:

- **East Texas**
  - Includes cities like Tyler and Lufkin, which are social and cultural extensions of the old South
  - Rural and biracial area (blacks and whites, with little of the ethnic diversity seen elsewhere). Predominantly black towns exist next to predominantly white towns (e.g., Tyler and Kilgore).
  - The economy of this area is centered around the cattle, poultry, and timber industries.

- **Gulf Coast**
  - Consists of cities like Houston and Beaumont
  - Very multicultural due to the constant influx of various ethnicities
  - One of the nation's most important shipping centers. The economy is based on industry and petrochemicals.

- **South Texas**
  - Consists of all towns south of San Antonio
  - Earliest area settled by Europeans
  - Primarily a bicultural region consisting of Mexican-American and Anglo-American culture
  - The economy is centered around ranching and agriculture.
  - Remains one of the poorest and most ecologically damaged regions in the entire United States and is deeply affected by the Mexican economy

- **Southwest Texas**
  - Includes the area around El Paso and Del Rio
  - Bicultural with characteristics similar to those of South Texas
  - The economy is largely based on sheep, goat, and cattle industries.
  - El Paso is the largest U.S. city on the Mexico border and has military, manufacturing, and commercial centers.

- **West Texas**
  - Includes towns like Lubbock and San Angelo
  - Socially and politically conservative, yet economically diverse
  - The northern area is primarily agricultural; the southern area is a major oil producer.

- **The Panhandle**
  - Socially and politically conservative
  - The focus culturally is toward Kansas City rather than the developed areas of Texas.
  - The economy is extensively agricultural, especially in grain production.
  - Important area for feedlots and livestock production

- **North Texas**
  - Dominated economically and culturally by the Dallas–Fort Worth Metroplex, which is the financial and commercial center of the state
  - Tends politically toward compassionate conservatism and moderate liberalism

- **Central Texas**
  - Triangular region shaped by Dallas, Houston, and San Antonio
  - One of the fastest-growing areas in the nation, especially the Austin area
  - Politically leftward leaning

⚬ A cultural and economic composite of all other regions; somewhat a microcosm of Texas culture

- **German Hill Country**
  ⚬ Slightly to the north and east of Central Texas
  ⚬ Includes areas such as New Braunfels and Fredricksburg
  ⚬ Remains culturally distinct
  ⚬ A conservative stronghold
  ⚬ The economy is centered on farming and ranching; however, wealthy urbanites have sought out the region's resortlike qualities.

The Republic

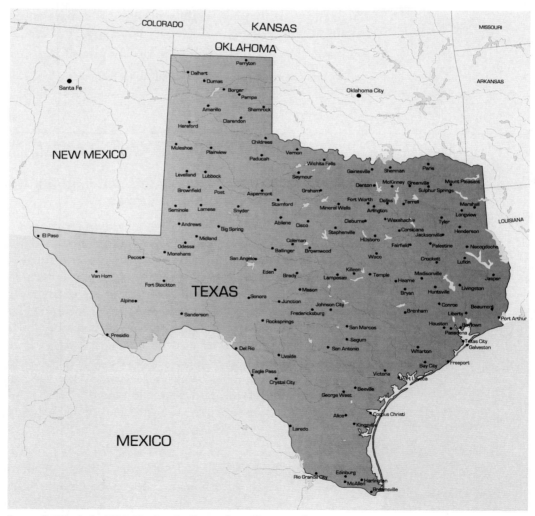

Image © Olinchuk, 2009. Used under license from Shutterstock, Inc.

In 1836 Texas gained independence from Mexico. The politics of that period were much simpler than now. Texans were not affiliated with political parties as they are today. Rather, the people coalesced around political individuals. Notably, Sam Houston was pro-statehood and advocated for peaceful relations with the Native Americans, whereas Mirabeau B. Lamar envisioned Texas as a nation extending to the Pacific and advocated for the elimination of the Indians.

Annexation

Texas voters approved annexation to the United States shortly after gaining independence; however, the slavery issue remained a sticking point until pro-annexation President James Polk's administration. On December 29, 1845, Texas became the twenty-eighth state.

Some unique features were incorporated in the annexation articles:

- **Texas retained ownership of its public lands, mostly because the United States refused to accept them as payment for Texas's public debt.**
- **These lands continue to produce millions of dollars in state revenues to the benefit of The Permanent University Fund and The Permanent School Fund.**
- **Texas was granted the privilege of dividing itself into five separate states.**

Source: The Treaty of Annexation–Texas; April 12, 1844. Retrieved July 9, 2009, at http://avalon. law.yale.edu/19th_century/texan05.asp.

THE TREATY OF ANNEXATION—TEXAS; APRIL 12, 1844

A Treaty of Annexation, concluded between the United States of America and the Republic of Texas

The people of Texas having, at the time of adopting their constitution, expressed by an almost unanimous vote, their desire to be incorporated into the Union of the United States, and being still desirous of the same with equal unanimity, in order to provide more effectually for their security and prosperity; and the United States, actuated solely by the desire to add to their own security and prosperity, and to meet the wishes of the Government and people of Texas, have determined to accomplish, by treaty, objects so important to their mutual and permanent welfare:

For that purpose, the President of the United States has given full Powers to John C. Calhoun, Secretary of State of the said United States, and the President of the Republic of Texas has appointed, with like powers, Isaac Van Zandt and J. Pinckney Henderson, citizens of the said Republic: and the said plenipotentiaries, after exchanging their full powers, have agreed on and concluded the following articles:

Article I

The Republic of Texas, acting in conformity with the wishes of the people and every department of its government, cedes to the United States all its territories, to be held by them in full property and sovereignty, and to be annexed to the said United States as one of their Territories, subject to the same constitutional provisions with their other Territories. This cession includes all public lots and squares, vacant lands, mines, minerals, salt lakes and springs, public edifices, fortifications, barracks, ports and harbours, navy and navy-yards, docks, magazines, arms, armaments and accoutrements, archives and public documents, public funds debts, taxes and dues unpaid at the time of the exchange of the ratifications of this treaty.

Article II

The citizens of Texas shall be incorporated into the Union of the United States, maintained and protected in the free enjoyment of their liberty and property and admitted, as soon as may be consistent with the principles of the federal constitution, to the enjoyment of all the rights, privileges and immunities of citizens of the United States.

Article III

All titles and claims to real estate, which are valid under the laws of Texas, shall be held to be so by the United States; and measures shall be adopted for the speedy adjudication of all unsettled claims to land, and patents shall be granted to those found to be valid.

Article IV

The public lands hereby ceded shall be subject to the laws regulating the public lands in the other Territories of the United States, as far as they may be applicable; subject, however, to such alterations and changes as Congress may from time to time think proper to make. It is understood between the parties that if, in consequence of the mode in which lands have been surveyed in Texas, or from previous grants or locations, the sixteenth section cannot be applied to the purpose of education, Congress shall make equal provision by grant of land elsewhere. And it is also further understood, that, hereafter, the books, papers and documents of the General Land Office of Texas shall be deposited and kept at such place in Texas as the Congress of the United States shall direct.

Article V

The United States assume and agree to pay the public debts and liabilities of Texas, however created, for which the faith or credit of her government may be bound at the time of the exchange of the ratifications of this treaty; which debts and liabilities are estimated not to exceed, in the whole, ten millions of dollars, to be ascertained and paid in the manner hereinafter stated.

The payment of the sum of three hundred and fifty thousand dollars shall be made at the Treasury of the United States within ninety days after the exchange of the ratifications of this treaty, as follows: Two hundred and fifty thousand dollars to Frederick Dawson, of Baltimore, or his Executors, on the delivery of that amount of ten per cent bonds of Texas: One hundred thousand dollars, if so much be required, in the redemption of the Exchequer bills which may be in circulation at the time of the exchange of the ratifications of this treaty. For the payment of the remainder of the debts and liabilities of Texas, which, together with the amount already specified, shall not exceed ten millions of dollars, the public lands herein ceded and the net revenue from the same are hereby pledged.

Article VI

In order to ascertain the full amount of the debts and liabilities herein assumed, and the legality and validity thereof, four commissioners shall be appointed by the President of the United States, by and with the advice and consent of the Senate, who shall meet at Washington, Texas, within the period of six months after the exchange of the ratifications of this treaty, and may continue in session not exceeding twelve months, unless the Congress of the United States should prolong the time. They shall take an oath for the faithful discharge of their duties, and that they are not directly or indirectly interested in said claims at the time, and will not be during their continuance in office; and the said oath shall be recorded with their proceedings. In case of the death, sickness or resignation of any of the commissioners, his or their place or places may be supplied by the appointment as aforesaid or by the President of the United States during the recess of the Senate. They, or a majority of them, shall be authorized, under such regulations as the Congress of the United States may prescribe, to hear, examine and decide on all questions touching the legality and validity of said claims, and shall, when a claim is allowed, issue a certificate to the claimant, stating the amount, distinguishing principal from interest. The certificates so issued shall be numbered, and entry made of the number, the name of the person to whom issued, and the amount, in a book to be kept for that purpose. They shall transmit the records of their proceedings and the book in which the certificates are entered, with the vouchers and documents produced before them, relative to the claims allowed or rejected, to the Treasury Department of the United States, to be deposited therein, and the Secretary of the Treasury shall, as soon as practicable after the receipt of the same, ascertain the aggregate amount of the debts and liabilities allowed; and if the same, when added to the amount to be paid to Frederick Dawson and the sum which may be paid in the redemption of the Exchequer bills, shall not exceed the estimated sum of ten millions of dollars, he shall, on the presentation of a certificate of the commissioners, issue, at the option of the holder, a new certificate for the amount, distinguishing principal from interest, and payable to him or order, out of the net proceeds of the public lands, hereby ceded, or stock, of the United States, for the amount allowed, including principal and interest, and bearing an interest of three per cent per annum from the date thereof; which stock, in addition to being made payable out of the net proceeds of the public lands hereby ceded shall also be receivable in payment for the same. In case the amount of the debts end liabilities allowed, with the sums aforesaid to be paid to Frederick Dawson and which may be paid in the redemption of the Exchequer bills, shall exceed the said sum of ten millions of dollars, the said Secretary, before issuing a new certificate, or stock, as the case may be, shall make in each case such proportionable and rateable reduction on its amount as to reduce the aggregate to the said sum of ten millions of dollars, and he shall have power to make a needful rules and regulations necessary to carry into effect the powers hereby vested in him.

Article VII

Until further provision shall be made, the laws of Texas as now existing shall remain in forge, and all executive and judicial officers of Texas, except the President, Vice-President and Heads of Departments, shall retain their offices, with a power and authority appertaining thereto, and the Courts of justice shall remain in all respects as now established and organized.

Article VIII

Immediately after the exchange of the ratifications of this treaty, the President of the United States, by and with the advice and consent of the Senate, shall appoint a commissioner; who shall proceed to Texas, and receive the transfer of the territory thereof, and all the archives and public property and other things herein conveyed, in the name of the United States. He shall exercise all executive authority in said territory necessary to the proper execution of the laws, until otherwise provided.

Article IX

The present treaty shall be ratified by the contracting parties and the ratifications exchanged at the City of Washington, in six months from the date hereof, or sooner if possible.

In witness whereof, we, the undersigned plenipotentiaries of the United States of America and of the Republic of Texas, have signed, by virtue of our powers the present treaty of Annexation, and have hereunto affixed our seals respectively.

Done at Washington, the twelfth day of April, eighteen hundred and forty-four

J. C. CALHOUN
ISAAC VAN ZANDT
J. PINCKNEY HENDERSON

Note:

That treaty was submitted to the Senate on April 22, 1844, with the presidential message of the same date (Executive Journal, VI, 257-61); and it was rejected by the Senate by a vote of sixteen ayes to thirty-five noes on the following June 8 (ibid., 311-12). Certain papers accompanied the presidential message of April 22, 1844, and also the sixteen later messages to the Senate of various dates from April 26 to June 10 (ibid., passe); from most of these the injunction of secrecy was removed during the Senate proceedings; nine of the messages of April and May, with the accompanying papers, were printed at the time in Senate Documents Nos. 341, 345, and 349, 28th Congress, 1st session, serial 435; of the first and last mentioned of those three documents (perhaps of the second also) twenty thousand copies were printed; but the message to the Senate of May 16, 1844 (Executive Journal, VI, 286-87), and the accompanying papers, the Senate refused to print (ibid., 287); with the other papers sent to the Senate they were made public with the presidential message to Congress of June 10 (Richardson, IV, 323-27; House Document No. 271, 28th Congress, 1st session, serial 444).

Civil War

During early statehood, politics revolved around pro-union and secessionist forces. When Abraham Lincoln was elected to the presidency in 1860, Texas voted to secede from the Union. Even though then Governor Sam Houston strongly opposed secession, he refused President Lincoln's offer of federal troops to force Texas to remain in the Union. Texas seceded from the Union on February 1, 1861, and joined the Confederate States of America in March.

During the Civil War, Texas supplied large numbers of troops to the Confederacy, as well as a lesser number to the Union. Texas also was responsible for the defense of the frontier at the Mexican border. As a result, the politics of the state during this period were quite militaristic.

Post–Civil War

Following the collapse of the Confederacy, federal troops occupied Texas and placed it under military rule. Sentiments running through the U.S. Congress at the time were divided between Republicans and Radical Republicans. Radical Republicans were a faction of politicians in the Republican Party between 1854 and the end of Reconstruction. They demanded harsh policies toward slavery and the Confederacy during the war and toward ex-Confederates after the war. The Radical Republicans also supported equal rights for freedmen. They were opposed by the entire Democratic Party and numerous moderate Republicans. Texas fueled the radical fire by passing black codes and electing former Confederates to office. With Radical Republicans controlling Congress, legislation was passed that strictly limited voter registration and the eligibility to hold office.

Governors between the end of the Civil War and the 1869 Constitution		
Andrew J. Hamilton	1865–1866	Provisional Governor appointed by President Johnson
James W. Throckmorton	1866–1867	Ran against Hamilton and was removed from office by Gen. Philip Sheridan
Elisha M. Pease	1867–1869	Republican who was appointed by Gen. Sheridan and served 2 terms as Governor in 1850's. Resigned because of differences with Gen. Joseph J. Reynolds. Considered the Reconstruction policies radical and despotic.

After the adoption of the 1869 Constitution and the election of Radical Republican Governor E. J. Davis, who fought for the Union, federal troops pulled out of Texas. For many Texans this was a world turned upside down.

The tenure of Governor Davis was one of the most controversial in terms of corruption. He maintained firm control of the state government and used the state militia to back him up. In 1873, the former Confederates were allowed to vote when the Radical Republicans lost power in the U.S. Congress. Governor

Davis was ousted from office in favor of Democrat Richard Coke. Davis refused to leave office, contesting the election based on the placement of a semicolon in the case *Ex Parte Rodriquez.* The "Semicolon Court" held that the election was illegal. The Democrats ignored the ruling, and the troops Davis had in place to protect his office ended up protecting Coke. Richard Coke took office January 15, 1874. On January 19, Davis resigned his office after President Grant refused his request for federal troops.

Texas Constitutional History

Constitution of 1836 (after independence from Mexico)	• Separation of church and state to the provision that clergy could not hold office • Limited the term of office for the executive • Reversed the Mexican anti-slave position and made it illegal for a master to free his own slave without congressional consent • Established a unitary form of government with no provision for states
Constitution of 1845 (written for the annexation)	• Exempted homesteads from foreclosure • Secured women's community property rights • Established a two-term governor and biennial legislature
Constitution of 1861 (written for the Confederate States of America)	• Very similar to the constitution of 1845 • Raised the debt ceiling • Prohibited the emancipation of slaves
Constitution of 1866 (written for readmission to the Union)	• Nullified secession • Abolished slavery • Renounced Confederate war debts • Very mild because the Republican Party was split in the U.S. Congress and the radicals wanted more punishment for the southern states
Constitution of 1869 (written to satisfy radical Republicans)	• Created a highly centralized government • All-powerful governor backed by the state militia
Constitution of 1875 (Constitution that is in place in Texas today)	• Reaction to radical Republican abuses • Cut salaries for officials • Restricted state borrowing • Gave little power to government officials • By denying the state power, gave little advance thought to the generations of Texans to come

Source: The Draft Constitution of 1874 and the Convention of 875. Retrieved July 9, 2009, at http://texaspolitics.laits.utexas.edu/7_2_7.html; and *The Handbook of Texas Online.* Retrieved July 9, 2009, at http://www.tshaonline.org/handbook/online/articles/CC/mqc1.html.

EXERCISE 1

Draw a timeline of Texas's several Constitutions, and briefly explain the provisions of each one.

EXERCISE 2

List five regions in Texas, and identify two characteristics of each region.

THE TEXAS CONSTITUTION

The Texas Constitution contains seventeen articles:

- **Article I—Bill of Rights:** Similar to the U.S. Bill of Rights, but since the U.S. Bill of Rights sets only minimum standards, the Texas Bill of Rights is longer and more extensive. This Article provides for the following:
  - Equal rights for women
  - Victim's rights
  - No imprisonment for debts
- **Article II—Separation of powers:** Separates the powers of government between the executive, legislative, and judicial branches. Additional amendments provide for checks and balances.
- **Article III—Establishes the legislative branch:** Specifies its structure and power.
  - Bicameral legislature with 150 seats in the House and 31 seats in the Senate.
  - Legislative session held biannually, once every 2 years in odd-numbered years
  - Sessions are limited to 140 days, which affects the passage of legislation.
  - Members originally were paid $5 per day while in session; today it is $118 per day. No other large populous state pays so little. The framers' intent was to give legislators incentive to keep sessions short, thereby not passing a lot of legislation and limiting government's authority.
  - Can call itself into special session. Special session is called by the governor to consider only the legislation that he or she presents.
  - Strictly limits the legislature in authorizing state debt
  - Confines legislature by making policies that normally would be handled by statute
- **Article IV—Establishes the executive branch:** The Texas Constitution establishes a plural executive by dividing executive powers among a number of independently elected officials, specifically the lieutenant governor, the attorney general, and the comptroller.
- **Article V—Establishes the judiciary:** The state constitution significantly fragments the court system by establishing two Supreme Courts:
  - Civil matters
  - Criminal matters

  Articles 3, 5, 8, 9, 11, and 16 all include provisions for local government, which contributes to the complexity of the Constitution.

  The framers guaranteed that even unimportant decisions that could be handled by the legislature are changed only by constitutional amendment.
- **Article VII—Specifies the amendment process:** Unlike the U.S. Constitution, the Texas Constitution may be amended by one single method:
  - An amendment is proposed by a joint resolution receiving a 2/3 majority vote in both the House and the Senate.

○ The secretary of state then prepares a statement that describes the amendment.

○ The statement must be approved by the attorney general and published twice in Texas newspapers, particularly those that publish official notices.

○ Ratification is by simple majority of those who voted. It can be put up for vote in either a general election in November by the numbered years or by special election determined by the legislature.

○ In 1980, the legislature began scheduling constitutional amendment votes in odd-numbered years when only local issues were on the ballot and voter turnout is typically much lower.

As of 2008 the Texas constitution has been amended 456 times. That is 16.9 times greater than the number of amendments to the U.S. Constitution. The Texas Constitution contains over 80,000 words; the U.S. Constitution contains about 7,500. Therefore, Texans say that the U.S. Constitution is a liberal constitution incorporating the basic structure of government and allowing the legislature to provide the details through statutes. On the other hand, Texas has a very restrictive constitution that incorporates detailed provisions in order to limit the powers of government.

Criticisms of the Texas Constitution

- Poor organization
- Numerous amendments
- Part-time legislature
- Legislative restrictions
- Plural executive
- Judicial structure and selection
- Local government structures and restrictions

The last time Texans tried to revise the state constitution was at the 1974 Constitutional Convention. The effort was highly and extensively touted, but it ended in failure.

Informative Websites

http://www.legis.state.tx.us
Texas Legislature Online

http://www.governor.state.tx.us
Office of the Governor

http://www.courts.state.tx.us
Texas Courts Online

Bibliography

Texas Politics: The Constitution. Retrieved July 9, 2009, at http://texaspolitics. laits.utexas.edu/7_printable.html#50.

EXERCISE 1

List and explain five articles of the Texas Constitution.

EXERCISE 2

Explain five characteristics of the Texas Constitution.

POLITICAL PARTIES AND ELECTIONS IN TEXAS

Republicans	Democrats	Libertarians
• Status quo • Traditional values • Stiffer penalties for criminals • Free market	• Change • Supportive of civil rights • Regulation	• Hands-off philosophy • Opposes social programs, taxation, and intervention in world affairs

The function of political parties in Texas as elsewhere is as follows:

- **To nominate and elect members to office**
- **To simplify the issues for the voters**
- **To mobilize and encourage participation by the electorate in election**

For more than a hundred years (1875 to 1975), the Texas party system was dominated by the Democrats. After 1975 the Republicans began making gains, and today they are competitive at all levels.

Political parties in Texas consist of a temporary organization and a permanent organization.

Party as an Organization

Permanent	Temporary
• Precinct chair • 2 county executive committees • County chair • State executive committee • State chair • Vice chair	• Precinct convention • County or senatorial district convention • June state convention

It is during the primary election that voters elect the precinct chairperson and, if they choose, serve as delegates to the precinct convention. The precinct convention is the grassroots of the party organization in the state. At the precinct convention, goals are set and delegates are selected for the June state convention, at which time, during the presidential election year the electorate is chosen and the state's primary platform is articulated.

EXERCISES

EXERCISE 1

List the characteristics of the party as an organization in Texas, both permanent and temporary.

EXERCISE 2

Identify and explain two characteristics of Republicans, Democrats, and Libertarians.

TEXAS GOVERNMENT: STRUCTURE AND FUNCTION

The Legislature

House of Representatives	Senate

• 150 members
• 2-year terms
• Requirements:
  • U.S. citizen
  • At least 21 years old
  • 2-year resident in Texas
  • 1-year residency in district
	• 31 single member districts
	• 4-year term
	• District lines drawn by legislature
	• Requirements:
	  • U.S. citizen
	  • At least 26 years old
	  • 5-year resident in Texas
	  • 1-year residency in district

Both houses are redistricted every 10 years based on the census; however, redistricting may occur more frequently, and that often happens.

Each session of the Texas Legislature is held for 140 days biannually during odd-numbered years. Special session may be called only by the governor to address his or her agenda and lasts for 30 days.

There are presiding officers in the Texas House and Senate, much like those in the U.S. Congress. These leaders:

• **Appoint most committee members and chairs**

• **Assign bills to committee**

• **Schedule legislation**

• **Serve as the chair and vice chair of the Legislative Budget Board**

The Speaker of the House is the presiding officer and is elected by simple majority of the House at the beginning of each regular session. The President of the Senate is the Lieutenant Governor of the State of Texas, elected independently and serving a 4-year term. The President of the Senate is the chair of the Legislative Budget Board and plays an important role in the fiscal policy of the state. Much like the committee structure that exists in the U.S. Congress, the Texas Legislature employs standing committees, subcommittees, and conference committees.

Agriculture and Livestock	Culture, Recreation & Tourism
Appropriations	Defense & Veterans' Affairs
Border & Intergovernmental Affairs	Elections
Business & Industry	Energy Resources
Calendars	Environmental Regulation
Corrections	General Investigating & Ethics
County Affairs	Higher Education
Criminal Jurisprudence	House Administration

Human Services
Insurance
Judiciary & Civil Jurisprudence
Land & Resource Management
Licensing & Administrative
   Procedures
Local & Consent Calendars
Natural Resources
Pensions, Investments & Financial
   Services

Public Education
Public Health
Public Safety
Redistricting
Rules & Resolutions
State Affairs
Technology, Economic Development
   & Workforce
Transportation Urban Affairs
Ways & Means

Source: Texas House of Representatives. *House Committees, 81st Legislature.* Retrieved July 9, 2009, at http://www.house.state.tx.us/welcome.php.

Process for House Bill   The following diagram displays the sequential flow of a bill from the time it is introduced in the House of Representatives to final passage and transmittal to the governor.

The Executive Branch

Governor of Texas	Powers of the Governor	Lietenant Governor

• **Requirements:**
  • U.S. Citizen
  • 30 years of age
  • Lived in the state for 5 years
• **Characteristics:**
  • 4-year term
  • No term limits
  • Salary of $155,345 set by the legislature
• **Legislative Tools:**
  • Veto
  • Line-item veto
	• Appoints members of state boards and commissions (all appointees subject to legislative confirmation)
	• Appoints the secretary of state
	• Appoints the adjutant general
	• Chief budget officer of the state (shared with the chair of Legislative Budget Board)
	• Clemency (in consultation with the Texas Board of pardons and paroles)
		• 4-year term
		• No term limits
		• President of the Senate
		• Chair of the Legislative Budget Board
		• Next in line of succession for governor

The Judicial Branch

Texas has a fragmented court system, and the distinction between civil law and criminal law is relevant. Civil cases involve private parties in which the remedy is some form of relief or compensation. Criminal cases deal with the commission of a crime and result in punishment upon determination of guilt. Original jurisdiction has the authority to hear the case for the first time. Appellate jurisdiction is the authority of an appellate court to review the decisions of a lower court.

EXERCISE 1

List the requirements to serve in the Texas House of Representatives and Senate.

EXERCISE 2

List and explain five powers of the Texas governor.

EXERCISE 3

Explain why some say that the Texas court system is complex.

CHAPTER

5 Ideology and Policy Process

I n the United States, public policy debates often dominate politics. Broadly defined, public policy is a choice government makes in response to an issue. Even a choice of inaction is a public policy. Every day, governments at all levels confront a variety of issues and must filter them by importance, then determine appropriate responses. Those responses become public policy.

IDEOLOGY

Ideology is a set of beliefs or a way of viewing the world. United States politics today includes two major ideological camps: liberals and conservatives. Usually, political liberals associate with the Democratic party and political conservatives associate with the Republican party. If such positions are put on a continuum from left to right, liberal Democrats occupy the left and conservative Republicans occupy the right.

Although these differences may seem insurmountable, most Americans do not fall on the far right or far left of this continuum. Most pick and choose among issues and fall somewhere closer to the middle. As depicted here, influential policy makers, politicians, and commentators occupy a variety of positions along this **scale.**

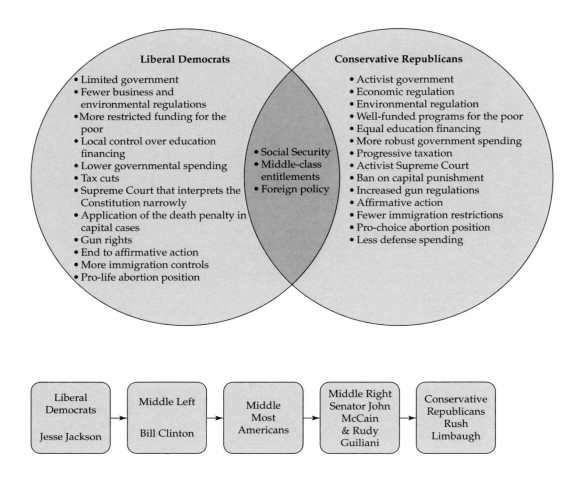

Because unanimity on far left or far right issues is rare, most public policy represents a compromise between the two. However, sometimes elections swing policy as a whole one direction or the other. For example, after Lyndon Johnson was elected president in 1964, policy tilted leftward. After Ronald Reagan was elected president in 1980, policy shifted rightward. Still, the ideological purists on either side rarely get everything they want.

POLICY PROCESS

The policy-making process in the complex U.S. federal system is often difficult to comprehend. A multitude of factors go into creating (or not creating) public policy. Generally, several events must occur for policy change to happen. However, these events do not have to occur in a rigid order. They sometimes can happen simultaneously.

Problem Identification
- Recognition of a problem or issue
- Awareness of the event
- Interpretation of it

Agenda Building
- Public Agenda—Mass Public
- Public knows about the issues
- Issues often get on the public agenda through crises, individual activism, technological change, media coverage
- Government Agenda—Institutions of Government

Policy Formulation
- Occurs when government actively considers the problem
- Both federal and state governments may attempt to address the problem through the legislative, executive, or judical branch
- Policy analysis—considers costs, benefits, and alternatives

Policy Adoption
- Occurs when an actual decision is made—when legislation passes, an executive order or administrative regulation is issued, or a court decision is handed down

Budgeting
- Key step for many policies to become reality
- If a program requires money, and money is not appropriated, the legislated action doesn't happen
- If a program is generously funded through the appropriations process, policy change may occur quickly

Implement-ation
- When goals and objectives are translated into an ongoing program
- To be truly effective, a policy must be implemented
- Often very political
- Sometimes more difficult than actually formulating the policy

Policy Evaluation
- When the policy is assed to see how it works
- Boring and tedious by definition
- Important because sometimes well-intended policies create unintended consequences

Factors Affecting Public Policy

The United States government is complicated, so many institutional factors affect the policy process. None of the steps in the policy process occurs in an institutional vacuum. Some of the factors affecting public policy include separation of powers and fragmentation, federalism, and incrementalism.

Institutional Factors			
	WHAT IS IT?	**HOW DOES IT WORK?**	**EXAMPLE**
Separation of powers	U.S. government rests on a principle of separate institutions sharing power.	Legislative, executive, and judicial branches may all have some effect on a particular issue.	Civil rights for black Americans was not received well in Congress in the 1940s and 1950s but was more successful in the executive and judicial branches.
Fragmentation	Each branch of government is fragmented	Legislative, executive, and judicial branches are each subdivided. Each part may have overlapping functions.	Congress is divided into committees and subcommittees. Many bills are actually referred to several committees simultaneously.
Federalism	The relationship between the federal and state governments	States retain some power of their own, which creates tension between federal and state governments in some policy arenas. Responsibilities and duties are clear in some cases.	Only the federal government prints money and provides defense. Education is more fuzzy—states and the federal government have a say.
Incrementalism	Step-by-step policy change	In the U.S. system, it is easier to change policy one small step at a time than to enact abrupt sweeping change.	It is less difficult to raise a tax by a small amount than to create a new tax.

Types of Public Policy

Some political scientists believe that policy type determines politics. Lowi (1964) created a typology that placed various policies in three groups: distributive, redistributive, and regulatory.

Lowi's Typology of Policies

Distributive
- Projects to benefit individual political districts: dams, water projects, etc.
- Easily given away
- Provide recognition for Congress members
- Do not create a clear enemy for the deprived (taxpayers in other districts
- Politics surrounding these policies are consensual

Redistributive
- Takes from one sector and gives to another—progressive income tax and social welfare policies
- Implemented through elaborate standards from a centralized agency
- Politics surrounding these policies are conflictual and ideological
- Class politics

Regulatory
- Controls economic behavior often through processes such as licensing
- Implemented through a large, decentralized administrative structure
- The indulged and deprived directly confront each other, resulting in conflict and compromise
- Political majorities constantly shift

Source: Lowi, T. (1964). American business, public policy, case-studies, and political theory. *World Politics* 16(4), 677–715.

Lowi's typology reveals much about policy formation, but like most typologies it cannot easily classify all policies. It is best used as a generic road map for studying specific public policies.

CONCLUSION

Political scientists and political practitioners usually study public policy by subject matter and often become experts in a certain area. Those with a personal interest could easily devote an entire career to researching and becoming an expert on environmental policy. Yet such a segmented approach can ignore the dynamic relationships among various policies. For example, immigration affects environmental policy because it exacerbates population growth. Tax policy affects the environment, too, because inheritance taxes can force heirs to sell off farm and ranch land to developers, contributing to urban sprawl. Failure to recognize policy relationships can result in myopic and unsuccessful policy solutions.

To create public policy, government makes a choice. This choice is forged in compromise and informed by ideology. The process of making policy involves several steps. Issues get on the agenda in multiple ways. It often takes a long time for significant change to occur, but sometimes political conditions are ripe for quick alterations. The complicated and decentralized political system creates a variety of factors that influence policy development. Separation of powers, federalism, and incrementalism combine to shape policy outcomes. Out of these processes emerge the public policies citizens deal with every day.

Informative Websites

http://www.nytimes.com/ref/washington/scotuscases_
AFFIRMATIVEACTION.html
Supreme Court Cases and Decisions on Affirmative Action (*New York Times*)

http://www.lib.umich.edu/govdocs/affirm.html
University of Michigan Affirmative Action Lawsuit

Bibliography

Lowi, T. (1964). American business, public policy, case-studies, and political theory. *World Politics, 16(4),* 677–715.

EXERCISE 1

List five characteristics of liberal Democrats, five characteristics of conservative Republicans, and the issues about which they usually agree.

EXERCISE 2

List the steps involved in the policy-making process and what is basically involved in each step.

EXERCISE 3

List the institutional factors that affect public policy and give examples of each.

6 | Regulation and Environmental Policy

A variety of public policies can be classified as regulatory. Characteristics of regulatory policy include the following:

- **Broad, vague legislation passed by Congress**
- **Implementation through one or more of the numerous independent regulatory agencies (also called boards and commissions)**

Since board and commission members are not elected, and those who work for them are often lifetime employees, they cannot be rewarded or punished through electoral politics. Fiorina (1989) believes this is very convenient for members of Congress since they can simply blame the bureaucracy when regulations are unpopular.

ENVIRONMENTAL POLICY

An environmental strain has long been present in United States politics. Thoreau in the nineteenth century and Teddy Roosevelt in the early twentieth century addressed environmental concerns. However, both emphasized conservation, not regulation.

Modern-day environmentalism began in the 1960s with the environmental movement, which began as a result of a variety of factors:

- **Obvious environmental degradation after decades of industrialization**
- **Growing affluence**
- **Rachel Carson's book *Silent Spring* (1962)**
- **The success of the Black Civil Rights Movement**

Choosing how to formulate environmental policy is quite difficult. Several difficulties confront environmental policy makers:

- **How to isolate individual polluters because of the nature of air and water**
- **How to create incentives to not spoil the environment because regulations have a significant cost for industry and consumers**

Interest groups play a role in environmental policy, particularly manufacturers, electric plants, and automobile manufacturers. Their incentive is to minimize costs, so they typically hope for fewer regulations. Once legislation is passed, however, they can often dilute regulations by co-opting agencies in a variety of ways. The mutually beneficial relationship that exists between an agency, a congressional committee, and an interest group is called an iron triangle (also sometimes referred to as a subgovernment or issue network). Ultimately iron triangles weaken the actual effect of many types of regulation.

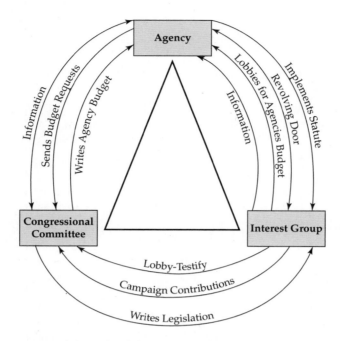

Ultimately the environmental movement was successful in urging Congress to address the problem. Between 1969 and 1973, many pieces of environmental legislation were passed. Overall, the spate of legislation passed and implemented in the wake of the environmental movement was successful in cleaning up some of the worst abuses. Most subsequent legislative amendments strengthened rather than weakened the original acts.

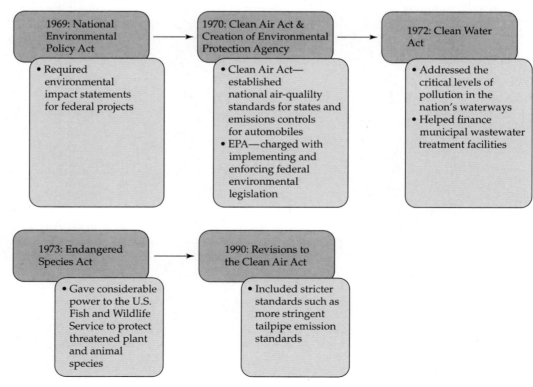

CONCLUSION

Today, some level of environmental regulation is a given. Many industrial processes have been improved to have less environmental impact. Recycling and conserving are more accepted culturally than in the past. However, numerous challenges remain, particularly in the international context. Many other countries, such as Mexico, are not as committed to cleaning up the environment as is the United States. Americans are affected by others' lack of policy (as when smoke from burning crop fires in the Yucatan blows into Texas) but cannot directly address it. Population growth in many parts of the United States continues to contribute to urban sprawl and habitat destruction. These problems are multifaceted and are much less likely to be solved in the context of environmental policy alone.

Informative Websites

http://www.ametsoc.org/sloan/cleanair/cleanairlegisl.html
American Meteorological Society: A Look at U.S. Air Pollution Laws and Their Amendments

http://www.epa.gov/regulations/laws/cwahistory.html
U.S. Environmental Protection Agency: History of the Clean Water Act

http://www.epa.gov/watertrain/cwa
U.S. Environmental Protection Agency: Introduction to the Clean Water Act

http://www.epa.gov/air/caa/peg/index.html
U.S. Environmental Protection Agency: The Plain English Guide to the Clean Air Act

Bibliography

Carlson, R. (1962). *Silent Spring.* Boston: Houghton Mifflin.

Fiorina, M. (1989). *Congress: Keystone of the Washington Establishment,* 2nd ed. New Haven, CT: Yale University Press.

Hardin, G. (1968). The Tragedy of the Commons. *Science 162,* 1243–1248.

EXERCISES

EXERCISE 1

Draw the Iron Triangle

EXERCISE 2

List and explain the pieces of environmental legislation that were passed by Congress between 1969 and 1990.

Domestic Policy

Domestic social policy includes a variety of approaches and programs, most designed to assist the most vulnerable members of society.

HISTORICAL OVERVIEW

For most of U.S. history, the federal government had a limited, almost distant, relationship to individuals, with many people viewing poverty as a character defect. Assistance for the most destitute largely came from other sources:

- **Churches**
- **County governments**
- **Charities**
- **Political machines (in some urban areas)**

The prevailing view of poverty as a character defect changed with the Great Depression, and the government's role did, too. Estimates vary, but unemployment soared at 20 to 25 percent. People who had worked all their lives found themselves jobless. This made the public more receptive to the idea that poverty could be a result of social forces.

Domestic social policy went through a period of growth during the 1930s in an effort to overcome the Great Depression and continued to grow through the 1960s and 1970s. Beginning in 1995 with welfare reform (Personal Responsibility and Work Opportunity Act), these policies have been scaled down. President Obama's 2009 stimulus bill could very well mark a change in this trend.

Poverty Assistance	
PRO	**CON**
Moral thing to do in a society as rich as the United States	Fosters a culture of dependency
Programs actually help people	Undermines work ethic
Redistributes wealth	Costly

Landmarks in U.S. Domestic Social Policy				
	PRESIDENT	**GOAL**	**WHAT DID IT DO?**	**EFFECTS**
1930s: New Deal	Franklin Roosevelt	Overcome the Great Depression	Created a plethora of social programs	Ushered in big government and the welfare state
1960s: War on Poverty	Lyndon Johnson	"Great Society"	Expanded and extended New Deal programs and created new ones	Government became committed to spending much more on social programs of all sorts
1995: Welfare Reform	Bill Clinton	Cut costs and improve effectiveness of social programs	- Turned Aid to Families with Dependent Children (AFDC) into Temporary Assistance for Needy Families (TANF) - Financed TANF through block grants to the states - Reduced states' financial incentive to add recipients - Gave the states much more leeway to restrict benefits	- In many states, the welfare rolls declined - Poverty rates were reduced - Household incomes of former recipients increased
2009: Stimulus Bill	Barack Obama	Overcome a deepening recession	Reinstated the financial incentive for states to add recipients to their welfare rolls	Remain to be seen

APPROACHES TO WELFARE

If the government decides to address social problems, particularly poverty, then a decision must be made about how that is done. The federal government utilizes a variety of approaches, and the U.S. system reflects all of them. To some extent this makes reform more difficult, as different programs have different goals.

Generally the U.S. government uses five approaches to welfare. Some are much more controversial than others, and all have advantages as well as disadvantages:

- **Work for welfare**
- **In-kind benefits**
- **Cash assistance**
- **Educational opportunities**
- **Economic development**

	WHAT IS IT?	POPULAR?	EXAMPLE	ADVANTAGES	DISADVANTAGES
Work for Welfare	Recipient must do something to receive the benefit	Yes	New Deal's Civilian Conservation Corps (CCC), which built infrastructure in many of the nation's parks	Politically popular because it is contractual	- "Make-work" projects - Displace private sector contractors
In-kind Benefits	Provide some kind of necessity like housing or food	Depends on benefit provided	Food Stamp program	Provides control over benefits used	-Significant bureaucracy and costs - In-kind programs are open to fraud, so government must implement measures to mitigate abuse.
Cash Assistance	Government sends a check to qualified recipients	No	Temporary Assistance to Needy Families (TANF)	Easier to administer because there is no need for fraud control	- No control over how the money is used - Some believe this type of assistance is detrimental to the work ethic.
Educational Opportunities	Government provides educational opportunities	Yes	Head Start	Very politically popular	- Very costly - Effectiveness is difficult to measure.

continued

	WHAT IS IT?	POPULAR?	EXAMPLE	ADVANTAGES	DISADVANTAGES
Economic Development	1. Cash assistance or tax abatements to private businesses or 2. Creating a pro-business environment through low taxes and reasonable regulations	Depends on political ideology	Urban Redevelopment Grants Local sales tax abatement Reaganomics	1. Popular with political conservatives 2. Requires little bureaucracy	1. Tend to favor new developments, and cash payments sometimes created unintended consequences 2. May not address specific geographic areas where the need is greatest, and racial or class biases may persist.

TYPES OF PROGRAMS

Americans are very ambivalent about social programs. Underlying much of the debate is a judgment about the "deserving poor" versus the "undeserving poor." There is more political consensus toward helping an individual who cannot control his or her circumstances than there is toward someone who has repeatedly made bad choices.

The politics surrounding social programs often depend on how the programs are set up. A program can be contributory or non-contributory. Social programs are also defined by their qualification criteria, and can either be means tested or non–means tested. In general, noncontributory and means-tested programs are more controversial than others.

Contributory	Non Contributory	Means Tested	Non Means Tested
• Recipients put into the program in some way • Example: Social Security retirement	• Does not require the recipient to contribute to the program or even ever have paid taxes • Example: TANF	• Require proof of poverty • Example: Food Stamps	• Provide benefits regardless of a recipient's wealth • Example: Social Security retirement

INDIVIDUAL PROGRAMS

Social Security Retirement

More Americans participate in Social Security for retirement than any other social program. It is a middle-class entitlement program and therefore does not generate the kind of controversy a poverty program does. In fact, most policy makers do not want to touch Social Security. Social Security is sometimes called the Sacred Cow or Third Rail of American politics: you do not kill a sacred cow, and if you touch the third rail you get electrocuted. Today this contributory program covers about 95 percent of the workforce.

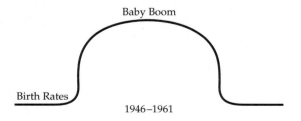

Social Security FAQ	
When was Social Security established?	In 1935 when Congress passed the Social Security Act
What is the goal?	To supplement income when family earnings are reduced due to retirement, disability, or death.
How is it funded?	A payroll tax on wages. Both employers and employees contribute to the tax: 7.65 percent for each, for a total of 15.3 percent on the first $106,800 (in 2009) earned; 1.45 percent of that goes to Medicare.
Where do the funds go?	Payroll taxes go into a special fund to be used only for Social Security recipients. Federal law requires that the surplus funds be used to finance the federal debt, but it is paid back with interest.
Who gets the money?	Workers can retire at age 65 and collect Social Security benefits if they have contributed, but the retirement age is going up for those born after 1958.
How much do retirees get?	Retirement benefits are calculated through a complicated formula that takes into account the number of years worked and the amount of money earned, with the number of years being more important. (Average retirement benefit in 2009 is $1,153 per retiree.)
How long do retirees receive the money?	Monthly for the remainder of a retiree's life.
What are the problems facing Social Security?	• People are living longer. The longer people live, the more the program costs. • Baby boomers will begin drawing Social Security in 2011. • The automatic cost-of-living increase (COLA) for beneficiaries greatly increases the overall cost of the program. • Any effort to curtail Social Security benefits, even slightly, is met with powerful resistance from the American Association for Retired Persons (AARP).

If Social Security continues in its present structure, future beneficiaries can expect to receive far fewer benefits than their parents and grandparents. Several policy reforms could address the problem, such as these:

- **Cutting benefits**
- **Raising payroll taxes**
- **Privatizing some aspects of the program**
- **A means test**

Each of these could help the situation, but each could also create problems. Currently, neither liberals nor conservatives want to seriously address the problem. For one thing, it is a future problem, and elected officials have more political incentives to focus on current problems, especially when solutions hurt.

In addition, the program itself bridges partisan reality by providing liberal benefits through conservative taxes. For now, Social Security continues to be the sacred cow of American politics.

Temporary Assistance for Needy Families

Temporary Assistance for Needy Families (TANF) is a means-tested cash assistance program. States receive block grants from the federal government to cover benefits, administrative expenses, and services. States have considerable leeway in setting requirements and restrictions.

Temporary Assistance for Needy Families (TANF)

- Prior to welfare reform it was known as Aid to Families with Dependent Children (AFDC).
- Most of the recipients are single mothers with children.
- TANF was designed to address concerns that AFDC fostered a dependent welfare culture and contributed to various social ills, such as illegitimacy. Gives states more discretion, imposes lifetime limits on assistance, and encourages work and two-parent families.

Welfare Reform

Pros	Cons
Welfare rolls have declined nearly 60 percent.	Other social services have been expanded to ease the transition from welfare to work.
The most employable welfare recipients exited the rolls.	Those who left often remain part of the working poor, in need of a variety of other programs.
Less direct cash aid is disbursed today than in the recent past.	The welfare state remains large and expensive.

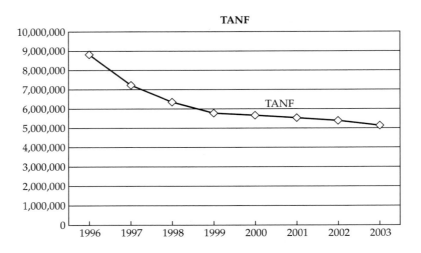

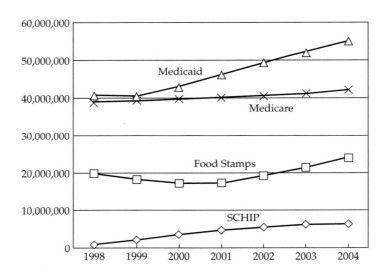

Health Care

Health care policy in the United States incorporates the private and governmental sectors. For both, rapidly rising costs present a major problem. A variety of factors drive rising costs, including these:

- **Increased longevity**
- **Advanced technology**
- **Third-party payers**
- **An increasingly litigious society**

Health care in the United States				
PRIVATE	**MEDICARE**	**MEDICAID**	**SCHIP**	**CHARITY**
• Typically health insurance through employers • Health care policy gets on the agenda more often when unemployment goes up • Organizational changes of insurance have helped to control costs	• Compulsory for Social Security recipients • A portion of Social Security payroll taxes goes to the program • Doesn't pay all health care costs • Has cost far more than originally envisioned	• Federal government sets overall standards and pays over half the costs for most states • States set their own guidelines for eligibility and services and pay the remainder • Much more comprehensive than Medicare • Means tested • Costs have far exceeded initial projections	• Like Medicaid, SCHIP is a state/federal partnership • Double-edged sword for states • Provides assistance to needy children whose family income is above the poverty line, but its costs are considerable	• Those without private means, insurance, or a government program often resort to a free clinic or hospital emergency room for care • Hospitals are stretched to provide care for nonpaying patients • Illegal immigration exacerbates this problem

Health care policy is complicated, incorporating a variety of interests, both public and private. Many on the left would like to see nationalized health care that would provide universal coverage for all, but such a solution requires high taxes and rationing and hurts existing insurers. Those on the right support continuing the current public–private mix and encouraging cost cushions, such as tax-exempt health savings accounts, but this solution does not stop rising costs or address the nonpayer problem.

EDUCATION

Education

- **Education remains primarily a state policy; however, the federal government has gradually increased its role in this arena.**
- **Everyone supports education—elected officials cannot lose when they tout education.**
- **Public education as a policy encompasses a variety of issues, such as curriculum, teacher training, religion, financing, state–federal relations, and appropriate discipline.**
- **Education is very difficult to evaluate. How do we measure educational success?**

Federal Education Programs Until 1965, the federal government was not significantly involved in K–12 education policy, although it did pass major assistance bills such as the GI Bill in 1944 and the Defense Education Act in 1958.

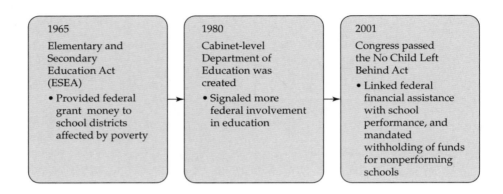

Texas Education Programs In Texas, the primary educational issue is financing. By state law, local school districts can only tax property (real estate). Tax bases of local school districts vary greatly; some encompass lots of high-dollar property and some lots of low-value property. This creates inequities in tax rates, and these differences have been the source of political controversy for decades. Several court cases have addressed this very issue.

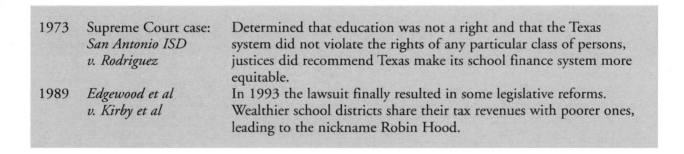

| 1973 | Supreme Court case: *San Antonio ISD v. Rodriguez* | Determined that education was not a right and that the Texas system did not violate the rights of any particular class of persons, justices did recommend Texas make its school finance system more equitable. |
| 1989 | *Edgewood et al v. Kirby et al* | In 1993 the lawsuit finally resulted in some legislative reforms. Wealthier school districts share their tax revenues with poorer ones, leading to the nickname Robin Hood. |

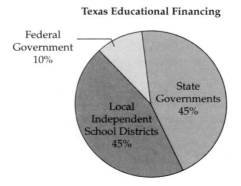

Texas Educational Financing

School financing is a difficult policy to address because electoral politics does not offer many rewards for solving it. Many Texas legislators are elected from legislative districts that include both rich and poor school districts. Either way they vote, the other constituency will be angry.

Unless the state totally funds education (no state does this except Hawaii), discrepancies in tax capacity will remain. It is unlikely this issue will cease to be a policy priority in Texas.

CONCLUSION

All levels of government participate in providing education, but state and local governments are most important. Taxpayers want accountability in education but also expect the schools to do more and more. Given that policy evaluation is difficult in this arena, few of the current education policy issues will be resolved soon.

Overall, domestic policy represents the issues liberals and conservatives often disagree on the most. Poverty and social problems are multifaceted and involve a variety of factors. Barring radical policy change, the U.S. system will likely continue a private, public, and charitable approach, and the arguments will revolve around how much of each is appropriate.

Informative Websites

http://www.aarp.org
American Association of Retired Persons (interest group for Americans 50 and older)

http://www.acf.hhs.gov/news/press/2006/welfare_rolls_decline_june_o5.htm
Centers for Disease Control and Prevention: National Center for Statistics

http://www.tshaonline.org/handbook/online/articles/EE/jre2.html
Edgewood ISD v. Kirby

http://www.cms.hhs.gov/NationalCHIPPolicy/
National Children's Health Insurance Program (CHIP) Policy

http://www.ssa.gov
Social Security Administration (home page)

http://www.ssa.gov/qa.htm
Social Security's future: FAQ

http://www.acf.hhs.gov/programs/ofa/tanf/index.html
about TANF
Temporary Assistance for Needy Families (TANF)

http://www.ed.gov
U.S. Department of Education

http://www.cdc.gov/nchs
U.S. Department of Health and Human Services

Bibliography

Edgewood et al v. Kirby et al, 777 S.W.2d 391 (TX 1989).

Morrison, I. (2000). *Health Care in the New Millennium: Vision, Values and Leadership*. San Francisco: Jossey-Bass.

Murray, C. (1984). *Losing Ground: American Social Policy 1950–1980*. New York: Basic Books.

EXERCISE 1

Explain the advantages and disadvantages of each of the five approaches to welfare.

EXERCISE 2

List and explain the five types of healthcare in the United States.

EXERCISE 3

List three characteristics of Social Security retirement.

8 Economic Policy

I n the United States, economic policy and electoral politics are closely linked. American voters often practice retrospective voting by rewarding or punishing policy makers based on the economy as a whole and their personal economic situation. While campaigning for president in 1980, Ronald Reagan asked voters a famous question: "Are you better off now than you were four years ago?" He went on to urge them to vote for him if they answered no.

The United States has a mixed economy: a capitalistic system with the government deeply involved in decisions that affect the economy. In addition, the government itself is a leading economic actor.

Americans are almost always interested in the economy, but economic issues get on the policy agenda largely through unemployment or inflation. The unemployment number is the percentage of the labor force actively seeking work but unable to find jobs. This percentage is never zero, but when it rises significantly the economy becomes a major issue. Inflation, on the other hand, indicates rising prices and wages and a decline in the real value of money. A classic definition is "too much money chasing too few goods." Inflation has more subtle effects than unemployment does, but they're just as detrimental. Typically, Democrats worry more about unemployment, whereas Republicans worry more about inflation.

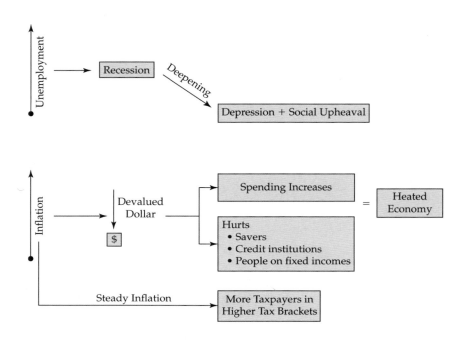

Liberals and conservatives have different ways of looking at the economy.

Economic Preferences of Liberals and Conservatives		
	LIBERALS	**CONSERVATIVES**
Approach to Stimulating the Economy	Keynesians, advocate government spending	Laissez faire, support tax cuts
How to Deal with a Cash Squeeze	Raise taxes	Cut Spending
Type of Taxes	Progressive taxes	Consumption (sales) taxes
Redistribution of Wealth	Beneficial	Unfair

Liberals and conservatives particularly disagree about wealth redistribution, which uses government to shift resources from the wealthy to the poor.

Wealth Redistribution	
PRO	**CON**
Avoids concentration of wealth	*Destroys individual initiative at the top*
Helps those at the bottom	*Erodes work ethic at the bottom*

The government employs four ways of making economic policy:

- **Monetary policy**
- **Taxation**
- **Subsidies and benefits**
- **Fiscal policy**

MONETARY POLICY

Monetary policy is the manipulation of the supply of money in private hands. Government accomplishes this through the regulatory actions of the Federal Reserve Board (the Fed). The Fed was created in 1913 and consists of seven members appointed by the president for 14-year overlapping terms. The president selects the chair of the Federal Reserve Board from among the members for a 4-year term.

The Federal Reserve Board manipulates the supply of money in three ways: open market operations, the discount rate, and reserve requirements. It coordinates policy so each method works simultaneously with the others.

Open Market Operations

- Sale of government debt (primarily treasury bills)
- Fed sets the interest rate the government pays to buyers of these financial instruments

Discount Rate

- Interest rate the Fed charges federal banks
- Other customers, such as people buying a home, pay more
- Fed operation most covered by the media

Reserve Requirements

- Percentage of deposits banks must keep on reserve
- Banks make money by lending money and charging interest, but government regulates the amount available for lending

These three actions influence the amount of money available in the economy. Often, although not always, there is a relationship between unemployment and inflation:

- **When unemployment is low, inflation is usually high.**

- **When unemployment is high, inflation is usually low.**

- **When unemployment and inflation are both high (which is rare), "stagflation" occurs.**

The Fed tries to steer the economy between the twin evils of unemployment and inflation by controlling the money supply. By controlling the three actions, the Fed can effectively reduce inflation or unemployment. Of course, the Fed does not operate in a vacuum; many outside factors influence these things.

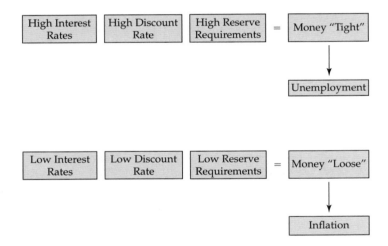

TAXATION

Government can influence the economy through taxation, not only to fund its own activities but also to encourage or discourage certain behaviors. A plethora of taxation choices face policy makers, from what types of taxes to utilize to what types of rates to levy.

The federal government utilizes a variety of taxes, including excise, inheritance, and payroll taxes, but its most important source of revenue is the personal income tax. This is a progressive tax, which means the percentage levied (the rate) increases as income rises. When politicians talk about taxes, including rhetoric about "middle-class tax cuts," this tax is usually what they are referring to.

2009

MARRIED FILING JOINTLY

Marginal Tax Rate	Tax Brackets	
	Over	But Not Over
10.0%	$0	$16,700
15.0%	$16,700	$67,900
25.0%	$67,900	$137,050
28.0%	$137,050	$208,850
33.0%	$208,850	$372,950
35.0%	$372,950	—

MARRIED FILING SEPARATELY

Marginal Tax Rate	Tax Brackets	
	Over	But Not Over
10.0%	$0	$8,350
15.0%	$8,350	$33,950
25.0%	$33,950	$68,525
28.0%	$68,525	$104,425
33.0%	$104,425	$186,475
35.0%	$186,475	—

SINGLE

Marginal Tax Rate	Tax Brackets	
	Over	But Not Over
10.0%	$0	$8,350
15.0%	$8,350	$33,950
25.0%	$33,950	$82,250
28.0%	$82,250	$171,550
33.0%	$171,550	$372,950
35.0%	$372,950	—

HEAD OF HOUSEHOLD

Marginal Tax Rate	Tax Brackets	
	Over	But Not Over
10.0%	$0	$11,950
15.0%	$11,950	$45,500
25.0%	$45,500	$117,450
28.0%	$117,450	$190,200
33.0%	$190,200	$372,950
35.0%	$372,950	—

Congress makes tax policy, but the president heavily influences its direction. Taxing income generates lots of revenue, but it requires a large, authoritative, and costly bureaucracy. The Internal Revenue Service (IRS) implements tax policy. The tax code is extremely complex; even the IRS sometimes misinterprets it.

To encourage certain behaviors, Congress allows tax deductions (reduces taxable income) or tax credits (reduces tax owed), which allow tax relief for specific actions. For example, home ownership is good for the economy. Homeowners tend to work harder, be more stable, and buy a variety of items related to the home. When real estate changes hands, realtors, attorneys, mortgage companies, title companies, and sometimes sellers all benefit. To encourage home ownership, the tax code allows a deduction for the interest paid on a home mortgage. The tax code is rife with deductions (and credits), some quite obscure.

Home Ownership versus Renting	
Starter Home in Central Texas	Two-bedroom middle-class apartment in Central Texas
Selling price: $180,160 Interest rate: 5.5 percent interest Term: 30-year mortgage	
Household income of $60,000; 15 percent federal income tax bracket	
Monthly mortgage payment: $1,485.68 (includes PITI)	Monthly rent: $824
BUT the homeowners can deduct $2,390 a year from federal taxes (mortgage interest and local real estate taxes)	
Owners build equity	Renters do not build equity

The personal income tax code remains controversial because top income earners end up paying the majority of federal taxes, whereas the number of people paying no income tax at all has increased significantly over the past decade. Although high-income earners have more disposable income, an emerging policy debate centers around whether or not it is wise to exclude large numbers of people from the tax rolls.

2009 Personal Income Tax Who Pays?

Top 1% of Income Earners	Top 10% of Income Earners	52% of Population	38% of Population
> 25% of Federal Taxes	> 50% of Federal Taxes	< 50% of Federal Taxes	0% of Federal Taxes

Source: Urban-Brookings Tax Policy Center, 2008.

SUBSIDIES AND BENEFITS

The federal government is a major player in the economy because it provides a vast array of subsidies and benefits that put money in the hands of those who otherwise would not have it. The following are examples of such subsidies and benefits:

- **Social Security retirement checks**
- **Food stamps**
- **Crop subsidies**
- **Defense education grants**

FISCAL POLICY

Major Steps in the Budget Process		
Formulation of the president's budget for fiscal Year 2010	Executive branch agencies develop funding requests and submit them to the Office of Management and Budget (OMB). The president reviews and makes a final decision on what goes in the budget.	February–December of 2008
Budget preparation and transmittal	Budget documents are prepared and transmitted to Congress	December 2008–February 2009
Congressional action on the budget	Congress reviews the president's budget, develops its own budget, and approves spending and revenue bills.	March–September 2009
The fiscal year begins.		October 1, 2009
Agency program managers execute the budget provided in law.		October 1, 2009–September 30, 2010
Data on actual spending and receipts for the completed fiscal year become available.		October–November 2010

Source: U.S. Government Printing Office
http://www.gpoaccess.gov/

Fiscal policy involves the federal budget, which allocates burdens and benefits. It is both an adversarial and a cyclical process. Technically, the federal fiscal year begins on October 1, but usually Congress has not yet completed a budget, so Congress adopts continuing resolutions until a final budget is reached, sometimes months later.

An important factor in the budgeting process is incremental budgeting. When government entities budget incrementally, they use last year's budget to create the next year's budget. To do so, agencies usually request a percentage increase, often more than they realistically expect to get, and bargain from there. Often political arguments about budget "increases" and "cuts" really involve the proposed incremental increase, not the actual budget.

Although this is an efficient way to calculate a future budget, it focuses political debate on the percentage increase rather than specific programs and creates an incentive for agencies to spend all of the previous year's budget in order to justify next year's requested increase.

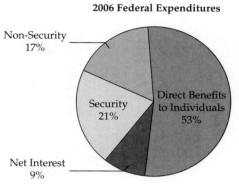

2006 Federal Expenditures

Source: Office of Management and Budget, 2008.

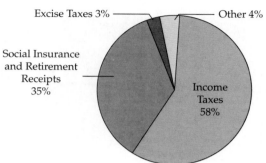

2006 Federal Revenues

Source: Office of Management and Budget, 2008.

Revenues and Expenditures

Budgets levy taxes and spend government money. The federal budget depends on income taxes, payroll taxes, borrowing, and excise taxes for revenue. Expenditures include direct benefits for individuals, defense (security), net interest, and grants to the states.

Types of Federal Revenue				
	PERCENTAGE OF BUDGET	**INCLUDES**	**WHO PAYS?**	**TYPE**
Income Taxes	58 percent	Personal (43 percent) and corporate (15 percent)	Falls heavily on middle- and upper-income earners	Progressive
Social Security Insurance and Retirement Receipts (Payroll Taxes)	35 percent	Mostly Social Security and Medicare taxes	Workers and employers	Social Security tax is capped at 6.2 percent on earnings up to $106,800. Medicare tax is fixed at 1.45 percent.
Excise Taxes	3 percent	"Sin taxes"	Producers of goods, consumers	Consumption

In addition to traditional revenue sources, the United States also borrows money for its budget. Borrowing in a single year is called deficit spending, and the total sum of money borrowed over the years is the federal debt. The government borrows money by issuing Treasury bills or U.S. saving bonds. If you own a bond, you have loaned money to the U.S. government. This source of revenue varies in significance from year to year.

Federal Expenditures

Types of Federal Expenditures				
	PERCENTAGE OF BUDGET	**INCLUDES**	**WHO RECEIVES?**	**TYPE**
Direct Benefits for Individuals	*53 percent*	*Social Security, Medicare, and Medicaid payouts*	*Individuals*	*Mandatory entitlements*
Security	*21 percent*	*Military expenditures*	*Defense agencies*	*Discretionary—hard to cut*
Net Interest	*9 percent*	*Payment of interest on government bonds*	*Bond holders*	*Mandatory— contractual obligation*
Non-Security	*17 percent*	*All other discretionary expenditures*	*States, federal agencies, etc.*	*Discretionary— easiest to cut*

Creating a federal budget remains an annual policy-making challenge. Depending on the partisan composition of the administration and Congress, the budget will allocate burdens and benefits designed to achieve a variety of policy objectives. The president's influence is significant, but Congress regularly alters the budget to reflect its goals as well.

TEXAS FISCAL POLICY

In Texas, the legislature holds most of the authority over the biennial budget. The governor writes a budget, but it is mostly ignored. The governor can influence budgets through a general veto or line item veto. This is a significant power, but

it is largely a reactive rather than proactive one. The governor's threat to levy a veto carries real weight because the legislature is usually out of session by the time the governor renders a decision, leaving no opportunity for an override.

The Legislative Budget Board (LBB), a joint committee with members from both the Texas House of Representatives and the Texas Senate, determines tax and spending policy for Texans. The speaker of the Texas House of Representatives and the lieutenant governor co-chair the LBB and have a significant role in selecting the House and Senate committee chairs that sit on the LBB. Therefore, much budgetary power accrues in these two individuals.

Unlike the federal government, Texas does not deficit spend: the Texas constitution prohibits it. Before the Texas budget can go into effect, the Texas comptroller must certify it as balanced. Texas can borrow money for capital projects such as highways or prisons, but it cannot borrow for basic governmental expenditures.

In general, Texas is a low-tax, low-service state. The states levies no personal income tax, and compared to other states social service expenditures are not high. In 2007 Texas ranked forty-seventh in the nation in terms of individual tax burden (Texas Public Policy Foundation, 2009).

Texas revenues are separated into taxation and non-taxation revenue. At about 25 percent of all tax revenue, the general sales tax is by far the largest source of revenue for Texas. It primarily taxes retail sales and a few services. At a rate of 6.25 percent, it is one of the highest state sales taxes in the United States. Liberal

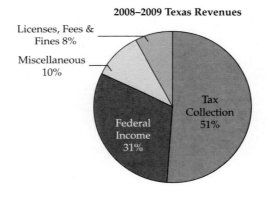

2008–2009 Texas Revenues

Licenses, Fees & Fines 8%
Miscellaneous 10%
Federal Income 31%
Tax Collection 51%

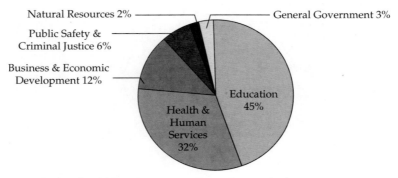

2008–2009 Texas Expenditures

Natural Resources 2%
General Government 3%
Public Safety & Criminal Justice 6%
Business & Economic Development 12%
Health & Human Services 32%
Education 45%

Source: Texas Ahead, Texas Economy in Focus. Retrieved July 9, 2009, at http://www.texasahead.org/economy/sb275/ecodevexp.html.

critics maintain that the sales tax is regressive—that is, that it falls more heavily on low-income earners. To mitigate the regressive nature of the tax, it exempts most food bought at grocery stores.

Texas's largest expenditure is education, followed closely by health and human services. The state's share of Medicaid costs constitutes a significant portion of health and human services spending.

In general, Texas is in much better financial shape than many states today. Still, the state faces financial pressure from illegal immigration, significant population growth, federal mandates for State Children's Health Insurance Program (SCHIP) and Medicaid, an education system challenged by performance expectations, and a decaying infrastructure. Some advocate additional taxes, including a personal income tax. Texas is one of the few states without one. A personal income tax would raise large amounts of revenue, but critics note that it would come with all the problems of the federal personal income tax.

CONCLUSION

Both the federal and Texas budgets are influenced by ideological politics. Liberals and conservatives have different budgeting priorities, so budgets typically reflect the group in power. Incremental budgeting puts spending pressure on both the federal and state budget systems, but they differ in many other respects. The U.S. president has a great impact on the federal budget, but the governor's influence on the Texas budget is far less. In Texas, the speaker and the lieutenant governor control the priorities as well as the process. Perhaps most important, the Texas Constitution forces Texas to exercise fiscal restraint, whereas the U.S. Constitution places no restrictions on federal budgets.

Informative Websites

http://georgewbush-whitehouse.archives.gov/omb/budget/fy2008/hist.html
Bush White House Archives (Budget FY 2008)

http://www.cbo.gov
Congressional Budget Office

http://www.irs.gov
Internal Revenue Service

http://www.taxpolicycenter.org/taxfacts
Tax Policy Center (Liberal Tax Group)

http://www.whitehouse.gov/omb
Office of Management and Budget

http://www.taxfoundation.org/research/show/1410.html
The Tax Foundation (Conservative Tax Group)

http://www.window.state.tx.us
Texas Comptroller of Public Accounts

http://www.lbb.state.tx.us
Texas Legislative Budget Board

Bibliography

Congressional Budget Office. (2009, April). *Historical Effective Federal Tax Rates: 1979 to 2006.* Retrieved April 20, 2009, from http://www.cbo.gov/publications/bysubject.cfm?cat=33.

Jones, B., and Williams, W. (2008). *The Politics of Bad Ideas: The Great Tax Cut Delusion and the Decline of Good Government in America.* New York: Pearson Longman.

Office of Management and Budget (2008, January). *Budget of the U.S. Government, FY2008.* Retrieved on April 20, 2009, from http://www.gpoaccess.gov/usbudget/fy08/browse.html.

Steuerle, C. E. (2007). *Contemporary U.S. Tax Policy, 2nd ed.* Washington, DC: Urban Institute Press.

Texas Ahead; Susan Combs, Texas Comptroller. (2008). *Economic Development and Business Development Expenditures.* Retrieved on April 20, 2009, from http://www.texasahead.org/economy/sb275/ecodevexp.html.

Texas Public Policy Foundation. (2009, April). *Fast Facts About Texas Spending.* Retrieved on March 7, 2009, from http://www.texasbudgetsource.com/fast-facts.

Urban-Brookings Tax Policy Center. (2008, June). *A Preliminary Analysis of the 2008 Presidential Candidates' Tax plans.* Retrieved on April 20, 2009, from http://www.taxpolicycenter.org/publications/url.cfm?ID=411693.

Urban-Brookings Tax Policy Center. (2008, August). *Distribution of Tax Units with Zero or Negative Income Tax Liability by Cash Income Level, 2009.* Retrieved on April 20, 2009, from http://www.taxpolicycenter.org/numbers/displayatab.cfm?Docid=1973&DocTypeID=7.

U.S. Government Printing Office. (2008, January). *Citizen's Guide to the Federal Budget: Fiscal Year 2001.* Retrieved on May 2, 2009, from http://www.gpoaccess.gov/USbudget/fy01/guide03.html.

U.S. Social Security Administration. (2009, January). *Update 2009.* Retrieved on April 30, 2009, from http://www.ssa.gov/pubs/10003.html.

Wildavsky, A. (2003). *The New Politics of the Budgetary Process,* 5th ed. New York: Longman.

Window on State Government; Susan Combs, Texas Comptroller. (2008).
Revenue by Source for Fiscal Year 2008. Retrieved on April 20, 2009, from http://www.window.state.tx.us/taxbud/revenue.html.

EXERCISE 1

List the major steps in the budget process and when they occur.

EXERCISE 2

Draw a pie chart depicting 2006 federal expenditures.

EXERCISE 3

Draw a pie chart depicting 2008–2009 Texas revenues.

EXERCISE 4

List the 2009 tax brackets.

Civil Liberties and Affirmative Action

C ivil liberties are the protections of individuals from government. For the most part, these liberties are guaranteed in the Bill of Rights, the first ten amendments to the Constitution. The courts are mostly responsible for making civil liberties policy. Although the bulk of policy is made through the states and lower federal courts, most of the focus is on the U.S. Supreme Court because it is the final authority on Constitutional matters. Civil liberties are some of the most divisive issues in U.S. politics.

Civil Liberties Issues

- Religion
- Free speech
- Protest rights
- Gun rights
- Criminal justice issues
- Privacy issues

The courts are responsible for decision making, but they have no enforcement mechanism. The U.S. Supreme Court, and all other courts, depend on other political institutions to enforce their decisions. Technically, a court decision only applies to the specific parties involved. Therefore, some decisions may be ignored. Often, compliance is voluntary and done out of fear of successful lawsuits.

NATIONALIZATION OF THE BILL OF RIGHTS

The Bill of Rights was written to protect individuals against federal power, but soon after its signing the Supreme Court entertained the question of whether or not the Bill of Rights could limit state and local government powers as well:

- *Barron v. Mayor of Baltimore* **(1833):** Federal bill of rights only restrains the national government, not the states or local governments.

- *Gitlow v. New York* **(1925):** Supreme Court reversed itself. It said that the speech and press provisions of the First Amendment could be extended to state and local practices through the due process clause of the Fourteen Amendment (ratified 1868). Thus the Court began a precedent of incorporating the Bill of Rights to the states. *Gitlow* also allowed the Court to spend more time on civil liberties cases.

Today almost every provision of the Bill of Rights has been incorporated to the states, so in effect state and local governments are bound by the national Bill of Rights.

Fourteenth Amendment	
Due Process Clause	**Equal Protection Clause**
"No State shall . . . deprive any person of life, liberty, or property, without due process of law."	"No state shall . . . deny to any person within its jurisdiction the equal protection of the laws."

DECISION MAKING

When the court makes decisions about civil liberties, they engage in a balancing act. No right is absolute. For example, a religious practice that demands human sacrifice cannot be accommodated. One cannot make a bomb threat and claim free speech. Generally speaking, the courts try to allow as much individual freedom as possible while still maintaining social order.

FIRST AMENDMENT FREEDOMS

The First Amendment addresses essential freedoms necessary for political discourse: religion, speech, press, and assembly. Although the explicit meaning of such clauses might seem clear, the court's interpretation of the implicit meaning can often be quite controversial.

First Amendment on Religion
"Congress shall make no law respecting an establishment of religion, or prohibiting the free exercise thereof."

The Constitution addresses two aspects of religion: establishment and free exercise. The establishment clause states, "Congress shall make no law respecting an establishment of religion." This means Congress cannot establish a "Church of the United States." In the eighteenth century most European governments supported an official church with tax money, so this was a significant departure for the United States.

The explicit meaning of the establishment clause is quite clear, but the implicit meaning is not. Do prayers in the public schools constitute establishment of religion? Do crèches on the lawn of City Hall constitute establishment of religion? Should religious symbols be placed in public places?

Prayer in Schools Court History

1962: Engel v. Vitale	• U.S. Supreme Court ruled that generic prayer written and approved by the New York State Board of Regents and recited daily in the public schools was unconstitutional because it promoted an establishment of religion, even if students could exempt themselves
1963: Abington Township ISD v. Schempp	• The court reinforced their decision, ruling that a state law mandating daily Bible reading in the Pennsylvania schools was unconstitutional
1971: Lemon v. Kurtzman	• The court developed a test for establishment of religion. Laws relating to church and state must have some sort of secular purpose, their primary effect must neither advance nor inhibit religion, and they must avoid excessive government entanglement with religion
1984: Wallace v. Jaffree	• The court ruled Alabama's statute mandating a moment of "prayerful" silence in the public schools was unconstitutional, but seemed to indicate the primary concern was the word "prayerful"
1992: Lee v. Weisman	• A 5-4 decision, the court ruled that prayers at voluntary public school events such as football games were unconstitutional because they coerced students into participating in religious ceremonies against their will
2000: Santa Fe ISD v. Doe	• In some school districts, students wanting prayers at such events led them themselves, often on a student-furnished PA system. In this case, the court banned these student led prayers, 6-3

Prayer in Public Schools	
PRO	**CON**
A simple prayer is NOT establishment of religion.	School prayer DOES violate the establishment clause.
School prayer helps instill a sense of morality.	School prayer is coercive; nonparticipants may be ostracized.
School prayer allows a religious minority to dictate school decorum.	Compulsory school prayer takes religious authority away from parents.

The Constitution addresses the actual practice of religion through the free exercise clause. The right to religious belief is absolute, but the right to practice is not. The Court decides free exercise cases on a case-by-case basis, with the goal of allowing as much religious freedom as possible while still maintaining an orderly society.

Speech and Press

Like religious practice, free speech and press rights are not absolute. Some forms of both can be restricted or even banned.

Free Speech and Press

Least Restricted	Highly Restricted	Not Protected
Political Speech	Commercial Speech	Obscenity
• Symbols can represent political speech ex. Flags	ex. tobacco products are not advertised on TV	

Assembly

Assembly rights, like religious practice, speech, and press, are limited, particularly in terms of place.

Freedom of Assembly Rights

No Freedom	Some Freedom	Greatest Amount of Freedom
Private Property	Public Facilities ex. public libraries, airports, etc	Public Forums ex. city park or town square

NINTH AMENDMENT PRIVACY RIGHTS

The most controversial part of the Bill of Rights is the Ninth Amendment, which addresses unenumerated rights. For the most part, the Court left the Ninth Amendment alone, until the court invalidated Connecticut's anti-contraceptive statute in *Griswold v. Connecticut* (1965). This case began the court case history of abortion rights.

Abortion Court Case History		
1965	Griswold v. Connecticut	Invalidated Connecticut's anti-contraceptive statute based on the right of privacy that is implied in the Ninth Amendment and the guaranteed rights emanating from the First, Third, Fourth, and Fifth Amendments.
1973	Roe v. Wade	Arguably the most controversial decision of the twentieth century. Roe struck down the Texas anti-abortion statute on the grounds that it violated a woman's right to privacy. This effectively struck down anti-abortion statutes in all states.
1973	Doe v. Bolton	Companion case to Roe, invalidated state restrictions on abortion on the same basis.
1989	Webster v. Reproductive Services	Court upheld Missouri's abortion restrictions. Webster was important because it signaled that the Court might approve more stringent restrictions. Several states immediately passed such laws.
1992	Planned Parenthood v. Casey	Court upheld abortion restrictions, which included a 24-hour waiting period. Many believed that this case would lead to the overturn of Roe, but little has actually changed since then.
2007	Gonzales v. Carhart	Court approved a congressional ban on partial-birth abortions in a 5–4 vote, but this procedure constituted only a small minority of abortions.

Ninth Amendment

"The enumeration in the Constitution, of certain rights, shall not be construed to deny or disparage others retained by the people."

Judicial Activism and Strict Constructionism

Controversy over abortion rights represents a deep schism in American politics that is manifested in a debate over the appropriate role of the Supreme Court in politics. Should the court play an activist role, interpreting the Constitution broadly in terms of implied meaning, or a conservative role, relying on a narrow interpretation of the document? This is actually an old question in American politics, but the early debates centered primarily on economic and regulatory issues rather than civil liberties.

Judicial Activists	Strict Constructionists
• Seek an expanded interpretation of the Constitution, particularly in the area of individual civil liberties • Support cases that enhance the rights of individuals rather than the state in criminal justice • Strict separation of church and state • Expanded free speech and protest rights • Extension of rights to gays, lesbians, and the disabled • Relatively unlimited abortion rights • "Rights-based politics" • Have faith in the policy-making capability of the court • Often believe that legislatures will not make the "right" policy because politically marginal constituencies are underrepresented in the electoral process • Political liberals who identify with the Democratic Party	• Seek a narrow interpretation of the Constitution, based on literal meaning or the Founders' intentions. • Believe the courts should not make policy, even if legislatures shy away from a particular issue • Want elected representatives, not appointed judges, to tackle the difficult issues in our society • Believe activist decisions such as *Griswold* and *Roe* take authority away from legislatures • Some argue that the decision that the Supreme Court made in the *District of Columbia v. Heller* (2008) case is an example of strict constructionism • Believe activist interpretations create slippery slope: Constitution means whatever is politically fashionable at the moment • Political conservatives who identify with the Republican party

Political differences between judicial activists and strict constructionists manifest themselves in politics in several ways, most notably in presidential judicial nominations. Typically, Democratic presidents nominate judicial activists and Republican presidents nominate strict constructionists. Policy activists care about these nominations because lifetime appointments mean a policy trend can last for many years, and the courts adjudicate some of the most controversial issues.

AFFIRMATIVE ACTION

Affirmative action represents one of the most controversial governmental policies. Affirmative action is particularly confusing because its meaning has evolved, and even today it is not always clear. Initially, affirmative action meant equal opportunity for minorities, but today it means special consideration. Most Americans agree with equal opportunity, but special consideration evokes more controversy.

Affirmative Action History

- **The Civil Rights Act of 1964 prohibited discrimination in employment, using contracting as enforcement.**

- **A series of executive orders from President Johnson mandated nondiscrimination:**
  - Department of Labor; Department of Health, Education, and Welfare (now Health and Human Services); and the Civil Rights Division of the Department of Justice were charged with implementation.

- **This policy quickly shifted to a results-oriented approach of goals, timetables, and sometimes quotas. All institutions receiving federal support were expected to comply.**

Challenges to Affirmative Action		
1978	Regents of the University of California v. Bakke	Court upheld affirmative action but determined inflexible quotas unconstitutional.
2003	Grutter v. Bollinger	Court upheld the University of Michigan Law School's admission policy, which incorporated race as one of many factors.
2003	Gratz v. Bollinger	Court struck down the University of Michigan's undergraduate affirmative program, which automatically awarded points for race, as "too mechanistic."

The court's ambiguity in affirmative action cases reflects the American people's ambiguity and also highlights the difficulty of implementing such a policy and accurately measuring success.

Affirmative Action	
FOR	**AGAINST**
Playing field already tilted in favor of whites	*Leads to reverse discrimination*
Creates tangible benefits for minorities	*Actually increases racial tensions*
Helps destroy stereotypes	*Creates perception of inferiority, undermines minority successes*
Compensates for past oppression and slavery	*Benefits go to middle-class minorities, not the most needy*

Affirmative action policy has also affected state politics. Several states have addressed affirmative action through referenda on state government affirmative action. In 2008, Nebraskans voted to ban affirmative action in their state and Coloradans elected to keep it.

Affirmative action remains a highly divisive policy. Most liberal Democrats are in favor of affirmative action, and most conservative Republicans oppose it. Although some have argued that affirmative action must end at some point, others see it as a public policy destined to remain in place for perpetuity. It shows no signs of dropping off the policy agenda anytime soon.

Informative Websites

http://www.aclu.org
American Civil Liberties Union (liberal judicial interest group)

http://www.judicialwatch.org
Judicial Watch (conservative judicial interest group)

http://www.usdoj.gov/osg
Office of the Solicitor General

http://www.supremecourtus.gov
U.S. Supreme Court

Bibliography

Morgan, R. (1984). *Disabling America:, the "rights industry" in our time.* New York: Basic Books.

Tribe, L. (1992). *Abortion: clash of absolutes.* New York: W. W. Norton & Co.

Wolfe, C. (1986). *The rise of modern judicial review.* New York: Basic Books.

EXERCISE 1

List and explain three characteristics of judicial activists and strict constructionists.

EXERCISE 2

Draw a timeline of the major court cases involving abortion rights

EXERCISE 3

List and explain three of the court cases pertaining to prayer in public schools

10 Immigration

In recent years immigration has been a hotly debated policy issue. Immigration is a complicated policy debate partly because it encompasses two forms: legal and illegal. Debates about immigration revolve around both cultural and economic issues.

IMMIGRATION POLICY HISTORY

In the early days of the Republic, the United States needed people, especially during nineteenth-century westward expansion:

- **Early nineteenth century: The majority of immigrants were Western European Protestant Christians.**
- **Late nineteenth century: Immigration numbers swelled, including more Eastern Europeans and Catholics.**

Regulating Legal Immigration: A Timeline

U.S. History of Regulating Immigration

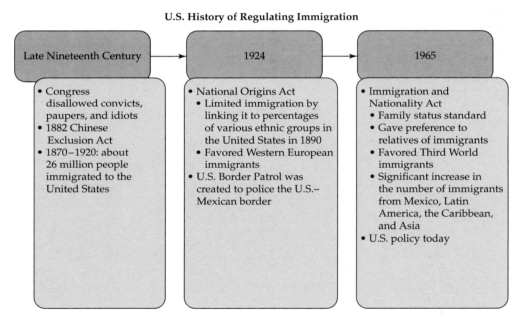

Late Nineteenth Century	1924	1965

• Congress disallowed convicts, paupers, and idiots
• 1882 Chinese Exclusion Act
• 1870–1920: about 26 million people immigrated to the United States
	• National Origins Act
	  • Limited immigration by linking it to percentages of various ethnic groups in the United States in 1890
	  • Favored Western European immigrants
	• U.S. Border Patrol was created to police the U.S.–Mexican border
		• Immigration and Nationality Act
		  • Family status standard
		  • Gave preference to relatives of immigrants
		  • Favored Third World immigrants
		  • Significant increase in the number of immigrants from Mexico, Latin America, the Caribbean, and Asia
		• U.S. policy today

Illegal Immigration: A Timeline

- **1980s**
  - Illegal immigration increased dramatically.
  - Most illegal immigrants came from Central America and Mexico and crossed into the United States from the Mexican border.

- **1986**
  - Congress granted amnesty to illegal immigrants who had resided in the United States since 1982.
  - Congress legislated sanctions for employers who knowingly employed illegal aliens. These sanctions were rarely enforced.
  - High numbers of illegal immigrants continued to enter the United States.

- **1996**
  - Congress beefed up border security, but this had little effect.

- **2005**
  - Congress did not pass President George W. Bush's proposed comprehensive immigration reform, which included greater border enforcement as well as a temporary guest worker program.

- **2006**
  - Immigrants and immigrant activists held demonstrations in cities across the United States, advocating legal status for illegal immigrants.
  - U.S. House of Representatives passed President Bush's reform measure.

- **2007**
  - Grassroots lobbying against the bill intensified.
  - Senate voted down the legislation.

- **2009**
  - Obama administration, combined with a more Democratic Congress, may reconsider the issue.

Illegal Immigration in the United States	
Number of illegal immigrants entering the United States	1990: 473,000 1995: 581,000 2000: 667,000 2004: 562,000
Number of illegal immigrants resident in the United States in 2008	11.9 million
Percentage of illegal immigration increase 2000–2008	42 percent

Source: Pew Hispanic Center. (2005, June). *Rise, peak, and decline: Trends in U.S. immigration 1992–2004*. Retrieved on July 10, 2009, from http://pewhispanic.org/reports/report.php?ReportID=53.

CURRENT DEBATES

Immigration is closely linked with many other policy issues, including the following:

- **Education**
- **Welfare**
- **Health care**
- **The environment**
- **The economy**

About the time immigration policy shifted from country-of-origin quotas to family status, the welfare state expanded significantly under President Johnson's Great Society. With a social safety net in place, the United States thus became a more attractive place for the poor and disenfranchised.

After the Civil War, the Fourteenth Amendment was passed to protect the rights of former slaves. It includes a birthright clause: anyone born in the United States is automatically a citizen. The United States is one of the few nations in the world with birthright citizenship. When family status replaced national origin as a legal immigration standard, having a child born in the United States became advantageous. The child automatically becomes a citizen, and the parents gain family status.

Fourteenth Amendment

Citizenship Clause

"All persons born or naturalized in the United States, and subject to the jurisdiction thereof, are citizens of the United States and of the State wherein they reside."

Other changes took place as well. Nineteenth- and early-twentieth-century immigrants were forced to assimilate, not only by physical geography but by general public agreement that imposition of the dominant Anglo culture was appropriate. Most of the immigrants themselves desired this, too (Schwarz, 1995). More recent immigrants encounter a more accommodating American culture, including a variety of native-language services. Hispanic immigrants have not acculturated as well as other groups and tend to live in more isolated communities. Fueled by high immigration and birth rates, such communities are increasing in size as well as isolation.

Electoral politics play a major role in immigration policy. Democrats support generous legal and illegal immigration policies because they want voters. In recent decades the majority of immigrants have been Hispanic, and Hispanics as a group tend to vote about 66 percent for Democrats. Many Republicans want curtailed legal immigration and strict border enforcement. However, a significant number desire liberal immigration policies because that keeps wages low, and low wages benefit big business. This political reality underscores most policy debates on the topic.

Should Immigration Be Curtailed?	
YES	**NO**
We have enough people.	*This country can accommodate an infinite number of people.*
Immigrants depress wages.	*This country was built on immigrants and we still need them.*
Immigrants displace American workers.	*Immigrants benefit the economy.*
Immigrants increase the cost of social services.	*Immigrants keep prices low.*

CONCLUSION

A variety of questions about immigration confront policy makers. Does the success of past policy models ensure success today? Should legal immigration be restricted? What kind of immigrants should we embrace? Should illegal immigrants receive social benefits? If so, to what degree? Should the United States accommodate immigrants through bilingual education programs and the like or revert to immersion/imposition? And finally, how many people should the country have? What is an optimal total population? Aside from partisan electoral considerations, what is best for the country as a whole?

Informative Websites

http://www.fairus.org/site/PageServer
Federation for American Immigration Reform (organization advocating limiting immigration)

http://www.weareamericaalliance.org
We Are America (pro immigration organization)

http://www.census.gov
U.S. Census Bureau

http://www.dhs.gov/ximgtn/statistics
U.S. Department of Homeland Security immigration statistics

http://www.ice.gov
U.S. Immigration and Customs Enforcement

Bibliography

Barone, M. (2001). *The new Americans: why the old melting pot works for the new immigrants.* Washington, DC: Regnery Publishing, Inc.

Buchanan, P. (2002). *The Death of the West: how dying populations and immigrant invasions imperil our country and civilization.* New York: Thomas Dunne Books.

Camarota, S. (2008, September 2). How many Americans? *Washington Post*, p. A15.

Pew Hispanic Center. (2005, June). *Rise, peak, and decline: trends in U.S. immigration 1992–2004.* Retrieved on July 10, 2009, from http://pewhispanic.org/reports/report.php?ReportID=53.

Schwarz, B. (1995, May). The diversity myth: America's leading export. *The Atlantic Monthly 275*(5), pp. 57–67.

EXERCISES

EXERCISE 1

List what the United States has done to regulate immigration over time.

EXERCISE 2

List the arguments for and against curtailing immigration. Take a position on the issue, and defend your beliefs.

11 Foreign Policy

Foreign policy encompasses the relations of the United States with the rest of the world. Unlike domestic policy, many factors in foreign policy making are beyond control. Domestic policy debates tend to be very ideological, with intense disagreement along partisan lines. Foreign policy is much less so; there is more partisan consensus on foreign policy than in any other policy arena.

President as Chief Foreign Policymaker

- Emanates from his powers of chief diplomat and other Constitutional abilities
- To make foreign policy the president relies on:
  - State Department—Secretary of State
  - Defense Department—Secretary of Defense
  - National Security Council—National Security Advisor
  - CIA and other intelligence agencies
  - A host of other advisors, both formal and informal

When the United States engages in foreign policy, the actions are often justified as being in the national interest. But the national interest can include many goals, including national security, economic prosperity, the spread of democracy, elimination of hunger, human rights, and so on. The two theoretical perspectives on national interest are the realist (or pragmatist) and the idealist.

Realists

Assume the United States is driven by economic and military concerns, and that such concerns may sometimes override human rights violations or other moral issues

Idealists

Prefer a human rights standard, banning friendly relationships with governments that grossly violate human rights

Foreign policy depends on a number of institutions and organizations throughout the world, including these:

- **Nation-states (the root of traditional diplomacy)**
- **International organizations such as the United Nations (UN)**
- **Regional organizations**
- **Multinational corporations**
- **Groups**

Although there are standard protocols for relationships between nation-states, no such rules exist for dealing with transnational groups such as Al Qaeda.

To implement foreign policy, policy makers use three basic types of approaches: diplomatic, economic, and military. Diplomacy is the most desirable, and military is the least.

Diplomatic	Economic	Military
Recognition	Development	Threat of war
Talks	Trade	Actual war
Agreements	Boycott	
Treaties	Embargo	

HISTORY AND DEVELOPMENT OF FOREIGN POLICY

Historical and Social Preconditions for Democracy and Modernity

Bourgeois traditions
Exposure to the Western enlightenment
High literacy rates
Low birth rates

Source: Robert D. Kaplan.

Preemptive War	
FOR	**AGAINST**
Deterrence	*Sets a bad precedent for other nations*
Defend regional interests	*Difficult to articulate to the public*

Isolationism (prior to World War II)	• Protected by two great oceans, the United States could effectively remain distanced from foreign conflicts
Containment (immediately following end of World War II)	• U.S. opposed the spread of communism, but did not want a full-scale war with the Soviets, so the U.S. embraced containment • Called for containing communism by isolating it and stopping its advances • American foreign policy went through several post war phases but containment undergirded all until the Soviet Union collapsed in 1991
Cold War (early 1950s to mid 1960s)	• Characterized by extreme tension between the United States and the Soviet Union, although there was never direct armed conflict between the two superpowers • Arms race between the U.S. and the Soviet Union led to a proliferation of nuclear weapons • U.S. adopted the military policy of Mutual Assured Destruction (MAD). This held that since both nations could render unacceptable damage to the other, neither would initiate hostilities
Vietnam Era (mid 1960s to 1970s)	• In the early 1960s, most Americans favored U.S. intervention in Vietnam and the troops were highly trained and motivated • By the late 1960s, public opinion had turned against the war • In 1973 Republican President Nixon signed a treaty ending the war, it did not hold and in 1975 North Vietnam invaded the South and took it over. The U.S. did not respond • Policy makers realized there must be a clear consensus on any policy resulting in numerous American deaths
Detente (early to late 1970s)	• Relations between the United States and the Communist world thawed and for a brief period, cooperative thinking replaced conflict thinking • Detente came to an abrupt end in 1979 when the Soviet Union invaded Afghanistan due to concern about rising militant Islamism and the desire to expand Soviet influence in Asia
The Regan Era	• Foreign policy agenda of "peace through strength" • Reagan prompted democracy as the best human rights guarantee • Mikhail Gorbachev assumed power of the Soviet Union. He liberalized the communist nation, encouraging a more free press and small doses of capitalism in the economy
Transitions to Democracy (1989–1990s)	• Chinese government began to introduce elements of a market economy and embarked on a policy of industrialization after a protest • A series of democratic revolutions in Poland, Hungary, Eastern Germany, Czechoslovakia, Bulgaria, and Romania toppled their communist governments • In 1991 the Soviet Union fell apart and reconstituted itself as a variety of different nation-states, some reflecting their pre-Soviet identity, with Russia as the largest and most powerful
Age of Terrorism	• The collapse of communism left policy vaccum in international relations and the world became a more complicated place • Countries transitioning from Communism to more democratic rule had many adjustments to make, and in some places, including Russia, levels of poverty, violence and corruption increased • Militant Islamism threatened stability in a variety of locales • The terrorist attacks on September 11, 2001 reoriented American foreign policy

CONCLUSION

Today the stark rationality of bipolarity and mutually assured destruction has been replaced by a multifaceted global situation with no guiding paradigm. Rapidly industrializing China is ascendant, financial markets are extremely volatile, nuclear proliferation continues, religious fanaticism remains a force in much of the world, and ethnic conflict erupts periodically. Al Qaeda leader Osama bin Laden remains at large. President Barack Obama faces a freer world but also one that is more complicated and less rational.

Informative Websites

http://www.whitehouse.gov/administration/eop/nsc
  National Security Council

http://www.un.org
  United Nations

https://www.cia.gov
  U.S. Central Intelligence Agency

http://www.defenselink.mil
  U.S. Department of Defense

http://www.state.gov
  U.S. Department of State

Bibliography

Kaplan, R. (1997, December). Was democracy just a moment? *Atlantic Monthly 280*(6), pp. 55–80.

EXERCISES

EXERCISE 1

Draw a timeline of the development of U.S. foreign policy.

EXERCISE 2

List the arguments for and against preemptive war.